Buyable

Your Guide to Building a Self-Managing, Fast-Growing, and High-Profit Business

by
STEVE PREDA

ISBN: 978-0-9984478-4-1 (hardcover)
ISBN: 978-0-9984478-7-2 (paperback)
ISBN: 978-0-9984478-5-8 (e-book)
· ISBN: 978-0-9984478-6-5 (audio book)

Published by: Amershire Publishing, Glen Allen, Virginia

Printed in the United States of America

Cover Design: Jason Anscomb
Text Design and Illustrations: Iram Allam
Editing and Indexing by Christina Palaia
Proofreading by Barry Lyons
Digital tools: Zoltán Ember and Yasser Hawas

To Dora, the love of my life and best friend.
Thank you for keeping our family on track to achieving our dreams.

CONTENTS

PREFACE

It was August 2011 and the European debt crisis was all over the news. Greece, Ireland and Portugal were on the brink of bankruptcy. Banks were running out of money and had stopped lending to companies. Stock indices were dropping and investors were pulling back from buying securities. Mergers and acquisitions transactions screeched to a halt because buyers had no liquidity, nor any confidence to make acquisitions.

This was terrible news for the business I owned at the time in Budapest, Hungary. At MB Partners, we helped small business owners raise expansion capital and attract international investors. All six transactions we were hoping to close that fall were interrupted, stopped until further notice.

My wife, Dora, and I sat at the dinner table in our vacation home at Lake Balaton, contemplating our future. The trauma of the financial crisis three years earlier was still vivid in our memories. In September 2008, I had attended a private equity investment conference in London, just after Lehman Brothers went into Chapter 11. That week the Bank of England had approved dramatic measures to save the UK banking sector, pouring £500 billion into it in a single day. The patterns unfolding in the financial sector then reminded me of what I had read about the tumultuous events that triggered the Great Depression in 1929.

On the flight back from London, I was seated next to the mergers and acquisitions chief of Deloitte, my company's biggest competitor, and we had discussed how the impending crisis could decimate our businesses.

At that time, I was convinced MB Partners was in a touch-and-go situation and that I had to cut expenses immediately to conserve whatever cash we had for the long winter ahead. The next morning, I downsized my team and eventually let go of seven of our 15 professionals. This dire measure had helped our company survive 2009 and rebound in 2010. By 2011, I felt like we were back at the top, en route to our best year ever. Then Europe plunged into financial trouble again.

"This Eurozone debt crisis is strike two for the business after the 2008 debacle," I told Dora. "Can we afford to wait for strike three?"

After dinner, I started researching options, and by the end of the weekend, we had decided that we would try emigrating to America.

In the spring of 2012, as we prepared for the move, private equity fund manager Krisztián Orbán called me. He suggested that our two firms merge and that we become partners and build a leading merchant banking operation in central Eastern Europe. I was flattered by his suggestion, but because Dora and I had already committed to move, I turned down his partnership proposal. I invited him, however, to make an offer for an outright purchase of MB Partners. The timing could not be better—I thought.

In hindsight, I wish I hadn't. His written proposal a few days later shook me to my bones. Krisztián offered to buy our fancy office furniture and computers but proposed only a fee-sharing deal for our transactions already in the works.

Further, he asserted, I was personally critical to MB Partners as CEO, rainmaker, dealmaker, newsletter editor, and public face as chief cook and bottle washer. I also was integral to the top-level investor relationships that drove the business, and with my departure, MB Partners would have no goodwill value.

I felt humiliated. After spending ten years advising business owners how to build "buyable" businesses, I got caught with my pants down. Worse still, we were facing a much harder transition to America without the full bank account I expected to have after selling MB Partners.

I wish I had had what I now call a Buyable Business because it would have given me options and flexibility. But the business was not buyable—there were no recurring revenues, predictable cash flows, or documented repeatable processes. Without me, there was no marketing machine or sales engine, and I had neglected to groom a management team to run the company. Though MB Partners was profitable, cash flow was choppy and the fortunes of our transactions could and regularly did change overnight. Valuing such a business was problematic.

The business was not sellable and it could not run without me. I had no other option but to keep steering the firm forward and try to generate profits while we settled in the New World. It made for a much trickier transition for our family of six.

I have written this book to spare you that pain. You can prepare well ahead of a transaction and create the options I didn't have by building a Buyable Business years before you need one.

INTRODUCTION

Are you an entrepreneur who runs a business that is not living up to its potential? Is your company growing and profitable, but not yet itself a valuable asset that can make you financially independent? Are you frustrated that you are not creating the kind of success that you dreamed of when you were first starting out?

You're not alone. According to Data Axle USA, 1.7 million businesses with 10 to 250 employees operate in the United States.[1] Statista, a leading provider of market and consumer data, reports that between 2015 and 2019 on average 21,000 mergers and acquisitions transactions occurred per year.[2] This means that if you own one of these businesses, there is a 1.2 percent chance your business will be sold within a year.

Further, an article in the *New York Times* quotes Gene Marks's Small Business Desk Reference in asserting that the average age of a small business is 8.5 years.[3] (Compare this with the average longevity of *Fortune* 500 businesses, which according to a 2019 McKinsey & Company report is 18 years.[4]) According to the Small Business Administration, small business longevity has been a stable statistic over the years.[5]

Taking the average small business life span and the chance of selling in any one year together, we see that there is only a 10.5 percent (or 1 in 10) chance that your business will ever sell over its lifetime.

This is a tragedy because running an "unbuyable" business means stress, frustration, and little reward to compensate its owner. In contrast, operating what I call a Buyable Business—a business that others would want to buy because they recognize its value and potential—allows you to enjoy the personal freedom of having a self-managing business. You can sell or harvest your equity in the company to support your personal purpose, the purpose you were put on this earth to pursue, and manifest the ideal lifestyle that you deserve to live. A Buyable Business is fun to run and develop. With it, you can create and nurture great relationships with like-minded entrepreneurs and build a worthwhile personal legacy.

If you are the owner or the CEO of a privately owned business that makes between $2 million and $50 million in annual sales, this book can help you improve the sad statistics I just shared. There is no reason that the 10.5 percent buyability rate of entrepreneurial businesses could not be doubled or quadrupled when owners take a systematic approach. I firmly believe that if you are intentional and smart about it, you can make almost any business buyable, which means you build it into a business that grows, matures, and flourishes beyond its predicted short life span while providing you with choices in how to harvest its gains. You just have to hunker down and implement the ideas and disciplines laid out in this book.

So, who am I to tell you how to build your business? Why should you listen to me?

I have spent more than 20 years helping business owners prepare their businesses for sale, finding buyers and investors for them, and coaching CEOs and leadership teams. I have assisted more than 250 companies and business owners in such endeavors and tell the stories of more than 40 of them in this book, using actual names and details of those who have consented to appear here. Along the way, I also share the story of how I made my own business buyable after all.

Throughout my career, I have been fascinated by the question of how Buyable Businesses are created. Some of my clients intuitively got it and built companies others wanted to buy, whereas many struggled with owning a business that found no willing investors. In several instances, my team would find only a single interested buyer to close a deal, while at other times, more than a hundred bidders were not enough to finalize a transaction. What made these businesses unbuyable?

There were always reasons for the failures, but rarely could I build a convincing case and articulate why one company was definitely buyable while another was destined to remain unsold, thereby trapping its entrepreneurial owner in an unwanted stasis. Figuring this out felt like a hit-or-miss process; often luck and timing appeared to be the most tangible factors explaining a business's success or failure. But I knew the answer had to be more specific and predictable than that.

My experiences over the past 20 years, first as an M&A advisor and later as a business coach and a curious student of management principles, led me to discover how any viable business can be developed into a Buyable Business. In 2016, I turned my raw ideas into a workshop for business owners, which I presented to more than 50 Vistage and other peer groups. Feedback, questions, and comments from hundreds of business owners and CEOs, including my coaching clients, helped organize my thoughts and experiences into the content of this book.

You hold in your hand the puzzle pieces I have put together for you. Each phase of creating and monetizing a Buyable Business corresponds to a profession I have practiced during my career, including management consulting, mergers and acquisitions (M&A) advisory, and business coaching. Thus, I feel uniquely positioned to paint a comprehensive picture of the "Buyability Process."

I am deeply passionate about helping you, the owner of a private business, turn your venture into a valuable asset that supports Your Ideal Life in and outside that business. I believe that as a business owner, you have a unique opportunity to make an enormous positive difference in the lives of your customers, your employees, your vendors, your strategic partners, and their respective families. Depending on your business, you can innovate new products, services, and processes; forge a talent-attracting culture; and establish a personal legacy. If you do some or all of these things, then almost certainly you will reap rich financial rewards for yourself and your fellow shareholders. Rewards are a normal by-product of creating value for others.

Building a Buyable Business takes some time, depending on where you are in the Buyability Process. You may have already created value and are ready to monetize it over the next 12 to 18 months. Or you may own a small business where you wear most of the hats and the business is worth next to nothing at the moment. In that case, you may need 5 to 10 years to build the business that can take you to your destination.

Rome wasn't built in a day either, and as author and start-up specialist

Gene Landrum lays out in *Entrepreneurial Genius*, even the most successful entrepreneurs of our time, such as Jeff Bezos, Steve Jobs, Bill Gates, Richard Branson, Michael Dell, and Mark Zuckerberg, took at least 15 years to break through.

However long it takes you to move your business to buyability, your journey will be shorter and more straightforward when you apply the principles you'll learn in *Buyable.*

This book is structured around the four parts of the Buyability Process.

Part One, Design Your Future, is about determining Your Ideal Life, that you want to live in your Next Chapter and what you need from your business to get there. What do you love doing the most? What fulfills you? What would you be doing with your waking hours if money was no object?

Once you understand how you want your future to look, you figure out how much it will cost to create or live the life you've envisioned. What does it take to get from where you are to where you want to be? How much business value do you need to create to achieve your goals?

Often, reaching your destination is more achievable than you think. Occasionally, you need to allow more time to accomplish this vision, or you might even need to rethink your plan. Sometimes you are already close and then I will invite you to envision much bigger goals.

Part Two, Orchestrate Your Business, is about arranging the moving parts of your business for optimal functioning. Are you applying each of The Seven Management Concepts to run your business well? Do you have the right people in the right seats and are you empowering them? Do you have a vision and a plan, and are you moving forward each week and each quarter, or are you driven by crises?

In this part, I walk you through 10 Management Blueprints that you can implement to shortcut the business orchestration process. We also take a deep dive and review selected Management Blueprint tools that help you implement the Seven Management Concepts.

In **Part Three, Drive Growth and Value**, you will lay the foundation that all Buyable Businesses must have in place to avoid scrambling when opportunity knocks. We will examine your business records, customer profile, assets, and contracts and make sure you structure everything properly from the get-go.

Then you will learn how to position your business in a "blue ocean" and remove all that could hold you back from revenue and profit growth. Next comes fine-tuning the engine driving your business.

When your company's value has reached orbit, you will groom the business for a transaction that harvests the value you want to take. The goal is to situate your business at its absolute best for when investors show up.

In **Part Four, Construct Your Ideal Life,** we come full circle. You now have a Buyable Business on your hands, and it's time to review your options for monetizing your investment, perhaps via a full or partial sale or a cash-out transaction, which allows you to keep full or majority ownership control. Depending on your goals, you will want to optimize the combination of company valuation, timing of cash payouts, and risks you retain, and I will show you how to evaluate your options and the implications thereof.

Then we review how a transaction unfolds and the critical success factors you can focus on and the pitfalls to avoid when harvesting your business.

This part wraps up by discussing the options you have during and beyond the transition, whether you stay in or leave your business—critical considerations because ultimately the whole Buyability Process is designed to help you live your ideal lifestyle and purpose.

Specifically, you will learn from this book:

- Why you need to build a Buyable Business regardless of whether you ever consider parting with it.
- The difference between proactive and reactive entrepreneurs and how their approach determines their financial and emotional success.
- How to design the ideal future state of your business, from which you can reverse-engineer the steps to getting there.
- How to determine your personal financial goals, which your business should help you achieve.
- How to estimate the value of your business right now and how you can determine the value your company must be worth in the future to allow you to harvest the cash you need for your Next Chapter— Your Ideal life.

- The Seven Management Concepts that you need to master to orchestrate your business into a well-oiled machine.
- What a Management Blueprint is, the major principles involved, and how to pick one that is right for you.
- How Management Blueprints can help you create the vision alignment, execution, and team cohesion needed to build a self-managing, growing, high-profit, and talent-attracting business.
- A recipe for building a solid structural foundation for your business so you avoid landmines that could impede its future buyability.
- What the major value drivers of your business are and how to engineer them into your company to create the most value in the shortest time.
- The ways to groom your business into a product that attracts investors and buyers who will value it highly.
- How you can harvest your business, with or without selling it, to achieve financial security, your desired lifestyle, and the purpose that drives you.
- What your potential future roles in the business are and how to pick the one that fits your needs and personality.

As the former owner of an M&A advisory firm, I sometimes feel a pang of regret for having sold some of my clients' businesses too soon. If I knew then what I know now, I could have helped dozens of entrepreneurs grow their companies further and capture for themselves more of the value that their buyers ended up harvesting instead.

However, you are now holding that crucial information in your hands and can use it to build a buyable and highly valuable business, which you may not ever want to sell. No matter the industry, if you have the desire to create an extraordinary company, this book can help you articulate where you're going, organize your business into a self-managing entity, engineer your value drivers, build a solid foundation for a transaction, and groom the business so that you can harvest part or all of the value that you have created.

Here comes the recipe as I discovered it. Welcome to the journey to your Buyable Business.

PART ONE:
DESIGN YOUR FUTURE

Create a life that feels good on the inside, not one that just looks good on the outside.

—ANONYMOUS

Part One of this book takes you on a big-picture thinking journey to discovering what you want your business to help you achieve and how you will build a Buyable Business.

It starts by defining what a Buyable Business looks like, including cul-de-sacs to avoid that lead to an unbuyable business. Then, we compare the opportunistic seller and the strategic seller using real-life case studies before reviewing the main types of reactive and proactive exits and how they emerge.

Next, we talk about different versions of an ideal life so that you can frame yours more easily, whether you remain inside or outside your business. We'll determine your Magic Number, what you will need to transition there. Then we take a look at your business and determine the gap between its current value and future desired value. You will know what it takes to bridge that gap over your envisaged time horizon.

Welcome to the Buyable Journey.

WHY BUILD A BUYABLE BUSINESS?

Don't wait for your ship to come in. Swim out to it.

—CATHY HOPKINS

In the late 2000s, Mrs. Juhász, the aging owner of an auto parts company I'll call PartsCo, phoned me. She was facing a life-threatening operation within the next 12 months, and she wanted to settle her affairs before the surgery, including selling her business. This was critical because she single-handedly managed the business and no family member was able or willing to step into her shoes.

At first glance, PartsCo was a glorious niche business. It was making about $10 million in sales, with almost half of that dropping to the bottom line. PartsCo dominated its niche; all its competitors were much smaller mom-and-pop shops. Some years earlier, its primary customer had offered to buy out the company and, when that fell through, tried to set up a competing subsidiary, which failed. The auto parts business relied on expensive equipment and skilled workers, which created barriers for new entrants.

The trouble was that Mrs. Juhász had never intended to sell, and she was now unprepared and under time pressure to do so.

Here are the issues she faced:

- The business was managed solely by Mrs. Juhász. She had some helpers but made all the decisions herself. Not a single engineer or even a college graduate was employed by the business who could have been elevated to a leadership role.

- PartsCo's financial records were a mess, handled by a semiretired bookkeeper she trusted, notwithstanding his incompetence and sloppiness.
- Mrs. Juhász's major customer trusted her and was wary of dealing with anyone else in her absence.
- That major customer generated an enormous part of revenues, and it would take years to diversify sales to eliminate the business's exposure to the risk of losing that customer.

These issues severely limited the pool of investors we could approach. No strategic or private equity buyers proved able to handle the financial and management issues or the risk of losing PartsCo's major customer. The business was virtually unbuyable.

The situation would have been different had Mrs. Juhász given herself two or three years to fix the business in preparation for a transaction. This would have been enough time to clean up the books and bring in and promote a successor or at least a talented individual who could run parts of the business without having to be micromanaged. Mrs. Juhász could also have cultivated new accounts to mitigate the concentration issue.

Because of the situation, we had to find an industry insider buyer who would be entrepreneurial enough to handle the issues and who had the experience and the reputation to maintain the buyer relationship. We also had to find private investors who would back the person leading the buyout.

The deal eventually worked out, but Mrs. Juhász received only half the price she could have harvested if her business didn't face avoidable issues that made it unbuyable.

But this shortfall wasn't her fault. She had never contemplated the concept of building a Buyable Business because she was too busy keeping her lifestyle business together and making as much cash profit as she could.

If Mrs. Juhász had built her business to be buyable, and if she had prepared for transition three, five, or 15 years earlier, she would have had a variety of options to choose from when her health challenge arose, such as stepping back from managing the business to be a passive shareholder or auctioning it to the highest bidder.

It is impossible to know with certainty, but I believe she could have made a lot more money on this sale. If only she had groomed the business in the 18 months prior to the transaction, she could have easily added 30–50 percent to the value of PartsCo. Had she mastered the basics (Chapter 7) in the prior three to five years, the business would have easily been worth two or three times more. And had she also engineered value drivers into the business (Chapter 8) in the previous 10 years, PartsCo could have been worth a multiple of the sale price paid for it in the fire sale Mrs. Juhász had forced herself into.

Read on to find out how you can do better for *your* business.

IS YOUR BUSINESS BUYABLE?

What Is a Buyable Business?

So, if Mrs. Juhász could have done better with a Buyable Business, then let's start by defining what a Buyable Business would have looked like for her and what it could look like for you.

A Buyable Business is an enterprise that others would want to own, a business that is worth more than the sum of its parts because it has goodwill value. Goodwill value accumulates when an entrepreneur increases the value of the assets in the business by applying vision, organization, and energy and by harvesting the ideas and efforts of a group of people working in or for the benefit of the organization.

A Buyable Business is self-managing—it manages itself without the involvement of the entrepreneur who created it. In contrast, when a new owner must replace the entrepreneur, the original owner still embodies much of the goodwill of the business, making the company unbuyable. In other words, the emperor is naked. That is where I was in the summer of 2012.

A Buyable Business is as or more profitable than its best competitors. Buyers like to invest in businesses that are making healthy profits, because these companies are more likely to offer differentiated products or services and to have competitive advantages.

A Buyable Business can attract top talent, which ensures that it remains competitive and keeps growing. Talented people make businesses grow so they can grow with them.

Would you consider your business "buyable" based on these criteria?

Let me guess: The answer is no. How do I know that?

At any one time, 90 percent of small businesses are unbuyable and chances are likely that yours is not as self-managing, profitable, and talent-attracting as you would like it to be.

But if you love your business and don't plan to ever sell it, why would you need to create a Buyable Business anyway?

This is the wrong question.

The right one is: Why would you ever want to create an unbuyable business? There seems very little upside in building a company that is not self-managing, not consistently profitable, not offering you options and flexibility, not growing, not generating predictable revenues and profits, a company that creates stress in your life, leaves employees unempowered, repels A players.

The only business that is worth building is a Buyable Business: an organization that runs on its own, grows, generates profits, manifests a great and talent-attracting culture, and offers differentiated products and services provided by happy and striving employees.

A Buyable Business is a successful enterprise that is going somewhere while attracting talented people and great opportunities into your life. Do you see any reason to build anything other than a Buyable Business?

Unbuyable Businesses

Yet, the great majority of businesses remain unbuyable. Let me give you some examples I have come across. I am ashamed that my M&A firm, MB Partners, represented several such companies. Earlier in my career, I didn't always recognize their issues and sometimes offered to help them even when I could not.

In the following sections, I describe the red flags that indicate when a company is potentially unbuyable. When more than one such red flag exists, a company needs immediate owner attention to save it from extinction.

In the Middle of Nowhere

Some businesses are located in an undeveloped geography, someplace difficult to reach that has little access to talent. I once visited a porcelain factory located deep in a remote forest with no inhabited areas near it. The plant could attract no qualified management and had to pay well above market rates to attract senior or even junior employees. The company has been surviving on government subsidies ever since, and remains in an unbuyable, government-enabled vegetative state.

Aging Workforce

Early in my career, I visited with an engineering business where the management bragged about their workforce having more than 30 years of experience on average. In reality, the company could not attract talent, and scores of its key people were planning to retire imminently. The business was fast running out of people, so what was there to buy? Managing the talent pool of a company is critical to ensure that the business remains vigorous, with good people feeding management succession and energetic young talent funneling in ambition and fresh ideas.

Poor Working Capital Profile

Some distribution businesses take on unsustainable risks. I have met several that paid up front for Far Eastern imports while delivering to their big-box customers just in time. This "strategy" requires ample working capital to fund the shipping and storing of inventories. Also, major retailers are often slow payers, which forces distributors to fund receivable balances as well. Such financing of high receivable and inventory balances could reach six to nine months of sales revenues in some cases, creating a ceiling on growth and spawning tremendous expense and risk for the owners.

These businesses are prone to go under in the next recession or upon the bankruptcy of a major customer or when shifting customer tastes make their inventories obsolete.

Lack of Documented Processes

Businesses without documented processes are at the mercy of their people leaving with the know-how in their heads. Worse, the lack of documented processes over time leads to inconsistencies, staff confusion, and costly errors. Buyers are not interested in acquiring companies that are at the mercy of a handful of key people who understand how the business works and who might leave after the transaction; often these people are the same as the owners, and that makes the company unbuyable. My former business, MB Partners, was an example of this before we implemented our Management Blueprints, of which you will read more in Chapter 5.

Buyers prefer companies that run on documented processes that are regularly updated and where each process is mastered by multiple people who can cover for the sudden loss or absence of individual employees.

No Recurring Revenues or Customers

Buyers of businesses love recurring revenues and value them highly. Unfortunately, not all businesses have or can create recurring revenue models, although many try. For example, construction companies are project driven, but they often sell maintenance or facility management contracts to generate recurring revenues. Professional services firms, such as law firms, rarely have recurring retainers, but they often have recurring clients who bring them billable work each year. Some businesses don't even have that, such as M&A firms, which have to sign new clients each year because very few of their existing clients have multiple companies to sell.

Buyers don't like businesses that depend on unsystematic business development efforts and will only buy them at a discount, if at all. On the other hand, businesses that have long-term or perpetual contracts are seen as sustainable, as long as they manage to keep client churn at a reasonable level.

At the Mercy of Customers or Vendors

High customer or vendor concentration can make a business be perceived as high risk. I represented a technology company years ago that earned more than 80 percent of its revenue from a global conglomerate. Even though this company's revenue came from 15 operating subsidiaries on three continents from more than two thousand relationships across the group, investors became alarmed and withdrew from investing in the business.

The same goes for a business that sources a large proportion of its products, raw materials, and services from one or two partners. This is called supply chain risk and can make a company unbuyable. Buyers are wary of situations in which the loss of a relationship can diminish 10 percent or more of the business overnight. They prefer businesses that have diversified away their dependency on individual customers or vendors so the loss of any one client doesn't threaten the company's viability.

Obsolete Technology

I once represented a printing company that supplied flexible packaging materials to blue chip, fast-moving consumer goods (FMCG) customers. The business was growing, profitable, and provided competitive products. We received an offer from a German strategic buyer, but the buyer abandoned the opportunity after noticing that the printing equipment was old and overdue for replacement.

Buyers are wary of businesses that require significant cash investment right after they're acquired. Beyond the unwanted monetary outlay, companies with run-down equipment are perceived as second-rate businesses, and buyers assume that old equipment is the sign of poor corporate health rather than conservative financial management.

No Internal Sales and Marketing Engine

Years ago, I advised a public relations company that provided excellent service and virtually never lost customers. Unfortunately, the firm had a weak sales process and the owner, who disliked hunting for business, could not attract reliable salespeople to join the firm. The company remained highly profitable until a major customer went out of business and a key executive left. After hiring a business development firm to no avail, the owner pulled the plug and took early retirement.

Having an internal new-business-generating engine is critical. Businesses that rely on good customer service for their growth or that outsource business development are not sustainable and are at the mercy of their business development vendors. Generating business is an indispensable core function of every company.

Selling Low-Margin Products

Low profit margins are toxic to a business's buyability. Buyers look for acquisition candidates with double-digit margins, as anything less implies commodity status and exposure to sudden shocks, such as a customer going bankrupt. A business selling at 5 percent profit margin will need 20 new customers to recover the lost receivables of a bankrupt customer. The owner is sitting on a time bomb. Furthermore, a single-digit profit margin is insufficient to fund investments in hiring, equipment purchases, and working capital that are often required for growth.

Fifteen years ago, my firm advised a prefabricated concrete manufacturer ("Prefab") that competed in a crowded market at razor-thin margins. Prefab's owner was a rainmaker, a well-liked manager who grew his business for over a decade until a nonpaying customer nearly bankrupted his company. Soon after, he died of a heart attack on the job. Low margins remove the buffer that can absorb inevitable mistakes and create constant stress. Bad for your health.

Exposure to Fluctuating Commodity Prices

Over the years we had several clients in the poultry processing business. Those companies oscillated between feast and famine as global supply and demand changes continually shifted poultry and feed prices on commodity markets. Two wonderful years when the poultry and feed prices diverged were often followed by a terrible one, when those businesses barely broke even, or lost money. Unstable profits kept investors away from the poultry sector, and strategic acquirers waited to pick off weakened competitors at fire sale prices or purchased retail brands from the receivers of bankrupted players.

Businesses that depend on un-hedgeable commodity markets are often unbuyable and only survive because their iron-fisted entrepreneur founder, sometimes with the help of government subsidies and grants, keeps them going.

Poor Financial Performance

Businesses are bought to make money. Investors and buyers seek profitable and well-run businesses that promise improving financial results. Poorly performing companies attract turnaround buyers at rock-bottom prices. Generating consistent and sustainable financial results is job one, without which a business is often perceived as unbuyable.

This is just a selection of issues that make businesses unbuyable. Unbuyability is the default position and where you'll find yourself if you're not intentional about building buyability into your business. So, let's turn to how it can be done.

Being strategic, instead of opportunistic, can make all the difference in harvesting the results of similar entrepreneurial efforts. In the following pages, let me share an example of each to illustrate the point.

ARE YOU STRATEGIC OR OPPORTUNISTIC?

An Opportunistic Seller

Struktoor was a construction company focused on major civil engineering projects commissioned by local and state governmental agencies, such as bridges, tunnels, river works, and flood prevention.

Two equal partners acquired and grew the company, one an industry insider engineer I call Sasha, the other a politician with money and connections; let's call him Ace. They grew the company rapidly by acquiring smaller competitors and amassing government contracts, and their business was highly profitable. Around 2006, they saw that the M&A market was hot and decided the time was right to sell the business.

They hired our firm to represent them and wanted to tie our fee to whether the sale price beat our valuation expectations. They insisted that we should get an unusually steep fee should we achieve an extraordinary valuation. I felt uncomfortable about this and suggested a flat percentage fee, but they questioned my commitment and trust toward them, so I played along, assuming that their target price was unachievable anyway.

Soon multiple offers came in for Struktoor and we signed a letter of intent (LOI) with the highest bidder, a global construction group (Gaffkont) for a purchase price of about $25 million. The next step was buyer due diligence to confirm the information we had presented in our sales memorandum and the customary deep dive into financial, commercial, taxation, and environmental matters that most buyers need before making a firm commitment.

The due diligence involved poring over data, documents, and contracts the sellers provided. A thoroughly prepared due diligence can be wrapped up in a couple of weeks, but it often drags out when all the information is not readily available.

Four weeks into the process, I sensed that Sasha and Ace may have been dragging their feet and asked what was bothering them. "The business has been doing better than we thought and we feel we should not sell at the agreed price," they informed me.

It is rare that a seller renegotiates soon after they accepted an LOI, but here it was, so I arranged a meeting with the buyers. We flew to Hamburg, where Gaffkont wined and dined us for two days. During the last meeting, the buyer's senior vice president, Erik, shared a parable about an Arab prince, with the message that this one time they would agree to changing the price, but we should not attempt it again.

Soon thereafter, the due diligence was complete, and we received a firm offer for $30 million. This happened at the end of the summer, and we started negotiating the sale and purchase agreement, but again progress was painstakingly slow. Struktoor's attorneys split hairs and challenged even customary contractual clauses.

I sensed something was amiss and asked for another meeting with Sasha and Ace. They informed me that their backlog continued to grow above expectations and that they had just completed the acquisition of a company that enjoyed a local monopoly on flood works in their county, which they expected to increase the value of the business. They felt that they would be squandering Struktoor at the agreed price and that we should get at least $37 million instead.

Again, I arranged another meeting with Erik, and after some wrangling, Gaffkont agreed to improve its offer. So much for Arab princes.

After that, negotiations gained momentum, and by the end of November we were close to concluding the deal. We set the date for signing the papers for Friday in early December. Our plan was to have Erik fly in for a last round of face-to-face talks and dinner on Thursday, after which we would officially ink the contract the next morning.

Sasha and Ace arrived at my office after lunch on Thursday and informed me of their decision not to sell Struktoor for anything less than $42 million. This year would beat profit expectations and they had the biggest-ever backlog for the following year, and so on and so forth.

My stomach sank. MB Partners' fee would be close to a million dollars and I was desperate not to lose this deal in the eleventh hour, but I doubted Gaffkont would renegotiate once again and just hours before the closing. What could I do to save the transaction?

Soon, Erik and his entourage from Gaffkont arrived, and I broke the news of my clients' new demands. They just about had had it and were ready to head back to the airport, but it turned out there were no more flights back to Hamburg that night.

Trying to break the icy atmosphere, I offered to take them for a drink. Dinner followed at an exclusive restaurant in the suburbs of Budapest, and then gypsy music and more drinks. At two in the morning, on the back of a napkin I suggested a compromise deal, and to my amazement, everyone agreed to it. I got home in the wee hours, feeling triumphant.

The signing would take place at nine the next morning, as planned, at the offices of Gaffkont's law firm. I arrived to find half a dozen copies of the updated sale and purchase agreement arranged around a vast mahogany table, with an army of attorneys and Erik's team in attendance. Sasha would be representing the sellers at signing, but he was not to be found.

He finally arrived 40 minutes late only to tell us he had one last condition on the sale: Gaffkont should give him a 50 percent raise in his role as the CEO of the jointly owned company. This was a shocking move, but Gaffkont was desperate not to leave empty-handed. They agreed to fund their share of the raise, corresponding to their initial ownership of 51 percent of the company. The rest, they said, should come from Sasha and Ace, as the 49 percent owners.

Sasha refused, arguing that he could not commit Ace to this deal and that Gaffkont should pay for his full raise. Discussions froze, then Erik and his team left in a huff.

The turn of events absolutely devastated me. How could this deal blow up after nearly 12 months of efforts round the clock to secure it? How would I get over losing a million-dollar fee, the highest ever for my firm?

I could not sleep for three nights, wracking my brain for ideas on how to resuscitate the transaction. Finally, at three in the morning on Monday, an idea struck me: What if I paid for Sasha's raise? It would cost half a million dollars over the next three years until the sellers were fully bought out. I could afford to pay for it from my fee, and our firm would still make

$500,000. We would be good with that.

I called Erik the next morning and found him to have cooled down after spending a relaxing weekend at his château. He was open to doing the deal if I could fund the sellers' share of Sasha's raise. I was on my way.

My next call went to Ace and Sasha, who were driving together in Ace's Ferrari. I quickly explained my idea of how I would waive half my fee to pay for Sasha's salary. After a few seconds' pause, which felt like an eternity, Ace started laughing uncontrollably.

"What is funny about that?" I asked in desperation.

"Steve, you didn't seriously think we would pay your fee, did you? Ha ha!"

Epilogue to this story: Four years later, Struktoor ran out of cash and went into administration. Sasha and Ace were convicted for bankruptcy fraud, although the judgment got eventually overturned on appeal in controversial circumstances.

The owners of Struktoor were driven entrepreneurs, but they had no apparent vision of what they wanted to build and why. They were attracted by opportunities and were always chasing the deal that looked most promising in the moment. Over time they lost their sense of proportion and started to believe in their invincibility. That blinded them and prevented them from seizing the opportunity to take their profits when they broke through the multiple business value targets they had set for our project. Sasha and Ace ended up losing their company and brushed close to losing their freedom, too.

Now let me share with you a very different story, one in which the owners of a business took a strategic approach to selling their company.

Strategic Sellers

Gulliver was a toy wholesale and retail business with annual sales of about $45 million and a healthy profit, founded by two best friends and Hall of Fame hockey players, Csaba and Péter. That is, Hall of Fame of Hungary, not the NHL, but they are two of the 10 "living legend" members of all time.

The two friends had married two sisters, Ildikó and Krisztina, and the four of them founded the company in the late 1980s. Over time, they became the management team of the business, and it was virtually impossible for an outsider to penetrate to the top tier of leadership. In the mid-2000s, they decided to sell the business and pursue their other passions.

The business was well organized with processes and ran on a sophisticated IT system. They led the market and were highly profitable; however, they made the most money selling Chinese imports to big-box retailers, which meant high receivables and inventory and minimal payables to fund it. A risky combination, as we discussed earlier.

But the sale of the business went like clockwork. MB Partners put on an auction and received half a dozen competitive offers. We sold the business by the end of the next year at full price. Péter stayed on the management team as Chief Operating Officer, but the private equity buyer still considered the company self-managed. Gulliver's team was perceived to be so well organized that they could hand over the keys, take full payout, and leave with minimal indemnities. The sellers even negotiated a long-term lease for the properties they kept ownership of.

But here is the best part: Csaba, after resigning as CEO of Gulliver, was elected as the president of the Ice Hockey Federation and helped the national team reach its best-ever ranking and remain at that level ever since. Another founder, Krisztina, was the first woman of her country to reach both the Arctic and the Antarctic and became a minor celebrity. Ildikó retired to spend more time with her grandchildren, and Péter stayed on at the company, which remained his passion, for several years longer.

The Gulliver team accomplished the transition in a way few business owners manage. They had a plan for the next stage of their lives, they knew what they had to achieve to get there, and they executed the plan. It required making their business buyable, and they sold Gulliver at the right time to the highest bidder.

They were strategic about their personal futures and leveraged their business to achieve their vision. The way to be strategic is to visualize your future and then to be proactive in taking the right steps to create it.

ARE YOU REACTIVE OR PROACTIVE?

The Default Setting

Unless you have a plan and execute on that plan, you are being reactive. Most entrepreneurs are reactive, even when they have mission statements and perform strategic planning.

Michael Gerber in his seminal book *The E-Myth: Why Most Small Businesses Don't Work and What to Do About It* speaks about the root of the problem.[6] The great majority of founders fall into entrepreneurship by being great at their profession and building a business around their own technical expertise. He calls these quasi entrepreneurs "technicians."

Unless these technicians work on their business as much as in their business they will remain stuck, limited by their personal technical capabilities. Gerber describes that the way to break through the ceiling is to transition to a "manager" role, delegating and getting things done through others, and eventually to "entrepreneur" status. The entrepreneur's primary role is to set the direction, find and exploit opportunities, and steer the ship.

Ascending to the entrepreneur role is a necessary but not sufficient condition, however, to make your business buyable. One reason entrepreneurial people start companies is for the freedom to experiment with whatever fascinates them. This tendency frequently leads the entrepreneur to chase "shiny objects" and jerk employees from one priority to the next, confusing and demotivating them.

I fell into the shiny object trap myself while running MB Partners. After the investment banking business took off, I launched a business brokerage operation to help smaller companies that could not afford our VIP service. I promoted one of my best employees to be the managing director of that venture.

While trying to get that brokerage business off the ground, I read *The E-Myth* and got excited about systemizing businesses into well-oiled machines. Soon I had a second shiny object to chase after and hired a senior executive to run that business.

By that point, I was devoting 60 percent of my time to these new businesses, and MB Partners started slowing down. In the meantime, the brokerage and systemizing businesses did not receive enough of my attention, either, and went nowhere. Instead of one growing and profitable business, now I had three failing ventures on my hands, with a bloated payroll and unhappy clients.

Six months later, I swallowed my pride and wound down both the brokerage and the systemization businesses. Painfully, I had to let go of my senior colleague, who was also a friend. My rising executive in charge of the brokerage got burned out by the experience and left our company. I learned a costly lesson about what happens when I react to exciting opportunities that don't organically fit into the core focus of my business. More on that later.

Let's review how being reactive can force you into an exit that does not serve your best interests, or one that unfolds with suboptimal results.

Reactive Exits

Whether you are proactive or reactive, at some point you will exit your business. Here are some scenarios in which reactive business owners leave their companies.

Ill Health

No one lives forever, and at some point, you will be forced to hang up your keys. It may be a dramatic event, such as a major illness or operation, like that of Mrs. Juhász, or you could have a heart attack or stroke on the job. Without building a competent team, it is challenging to pull back and dial down the stress of running the company during times of ill health. You need to grow the business so that you can afford a team and then train them so that you build a self-managing organization that can operate without you if necessary or desirable.

Burnout

If illness doesn't throw you off your feet, you may as well burn yourself out. A business is either driven by a compelling vision or by the fear of failure. The latter is the default setting. It is human nature to relax and coast when your bank balance is high.

Predictably, coasting puts the brakes on your momentum, triggering a slide and a crisis. This, in turn, reignites your survival instinct, and you will pull yourself together. The crisis mobilizes all your resources and you run on adrenaline for a while. However, you cannot sustain this level of fear-induced intensity, and you will feel the need to relax again as soon as your business has recovered.

Most companies are living this stop–go cycle, and they stumble from one crisis to another, only making enough money to pay their bills and stay in business. It takes effort, and planning, to leave the gravitational force of the survival zone. However, after take-off, sustained effort creates the momentum to propel you forward, like when a plane becomes airborne. Eventually, you reach cruising altitude and need to put in less effort going forward, which is what happens when you have created a self-managing business.

Indebtedness

Borrowing is a slippery slope for a small business, because banks tend to lend for the wrong reasons. A growing business needs to invest in productive assets, predominantly people, marketing, and product development. (Hard equipment and vehicles can often be leased.) Banks don't like to fund off-balance-sheet assets because these can fast lose their value when a business becomes unable to service its loans.

Therefore banks prefer to push loans secured by the personal property and creditworthiness of the business owner, and they like to lend against assets they can better control and liquidate, such as receivables and inventories. One of my clients, a construction services company, prefers not to collect on receivables early because its bank would reduce its credit line to align with the lower "collateral balance." Similarly, banks incentivize the buildup of inventories by lending against them, whether or not that is in the best interest of the business.

Unfortunately, borrowing against receivables and inventories can be a self-defeating strategy. If you don't generate enough profit margin to finance your growing working capital needs, then your business model is flawed and you should fix it as soon as possible. Solutions include collecting up-front payments and engineering a just-in-time delivery system.

"But what if all my competitors are offering terms and are willing to keep inventories?" you ask. Then you are in a commodity business, which is a dangerous place to be. The users of commodities tend to be price driven and fickle. You need to break out of commodity status by providing more valuable products or services or by tailoring your offerings to a niche market if you want to build a Buyable Business.

Slipping into bank debt and financing growth with credit lines means that you're generating paper profits, much of which is eaten up by your growing working capital needs, which leaves little cash available in the business for dividends or growth. Serving commodity markets is not a scalable business model and you will not accumulate much equity in your company. More on that later. Structurally indebted companies are also unattractive to buyers.

Partnership Dysfunction

A healthy team and working capital profile are important, but not sufficient to make your business viable. The relations between partners and owners also need to be healthy.

Perfect business partnerships are rare. It is the exception, not the rule, for partners to complement each other, grow as leaders at a similar pace, and maintain compatible long-term aspirations. More often than not, one partner ends up playing a bigger part because of their superior drive, energy, or talent to attract and motivate people.

Equal partnerships are risky because they can put a damper on growth when the more active partner becomes bitter about pulling the cart on behalf of their less-driven or less-effective fellow owners. In such situations, partners sometimes agree to adjust their equity holdings to reflect their contributions to the business. But often they cannot find a mutually satisfactory solution and end up dissolving their partnership by splitting the business in the middle or by one partner buying out the other.

In each of these examples, outside circumstances force the business owner into leaving the business. Next we will review how being proactive helps you reach better outcomes.

Proactive Exits

Opening a Compelling Next Chapter

As you recall from the earlier story, the founders of the toy company Gulliver initiated an exit so that they could fulfill their desires. Gulliver was built to be buyable, and selling 100 percent of the company for cash allowed Csaba to pursue his passion for ice hockey, Krisztina to conquer the Arctic and the Antarctic, and Ildikó to lavish time and attention on her family. It is rare for multiple owners to have in mind desirable missions outside the business, especially for them to realize it all at the same time. Businesses that are owned by a sole entrepreneur who engineers an exit and businesses in which one or more incumbents acquire the stake of another founder are more frequent.

I discuss examples of worthwhile postentrepreneurial careers in the next chapter.

Starting Another Business

Certain entrepreneurs realize that they enjoy and have the talent to build a business to a certain size, after which they lose interest. Exiting their current business allows them to become financially independent and creates the starting capital to launch another business that may have more potential.

I know of an engineering company that had grown to more than a hundred people when the owners decided there was limited upside in continuing to build a business that depended on selling consultant hours. They incubated a software services business on the side. Selling the consulting business helped them eliminate their personal debts and financial guarantees, take chips off the table, and capitalize a technology startup they had spun off.

Then they turned their tech spin-off into a Software as a Service (SaaS) company, which is much more scalable than the consulting business ever was.

Also consider the case of Linda Nash, a serial business angel who incubates new businesses to sell them off as soon as they have become viable, with stable revenues and independent management, typically after two or three years. More on her later.

Family and/or Management Succession

Perpetuating family businesses through multiple generations is challenging. According to the Family Business Network, a nonprofit serving the owners and leaders of family-owned businesses, one out of three family companies pull off a successful family succession, and only 3 percent of family companies last for four generations or beyond. The oldest family business is the Hoshi Ryokan Hotel, founded in the year 718 and being run by the 46th generation[7] of the family. Japan hosts 60 percent of the 5,000 family companies worldwide that are more than 200 years old. Most of them survived by adhering to and perpetuating fundamental family values.

One family company that created a proactive succession is Szabadics, a civil engineering company in western Hungary founded by József Szabadics. József built a Buyable Business and facilitated a smooth ownership transition to his two sons, Zoltán and Attila. They did this while creating personal liquidity for the founder and his two sons and expanding the management team with two senior executives, one of whom became the CEO of the company.

In a single transaction, József cashed out 60 percent of the equity of the business and arranged a management transition to an independent CEO, while keeping his two sons engaged in a thus institutionalized business. The Szabadics family retained 90 percent ownership in the business. See more about this transaction in Chapter 10.

Since the transaction, Szabadics grew the number of its employees fourfold, and the small-town company expanded its geographical footprint to cover 50 percent of western Hungary. The company has a multi-layer leadership structure and can attract and keep talent by continually growing and offering a career structure to its employees.

Szabadics achieved the family and management transitions at the same time, which is rare. Occasionally, an owner can sell the business to their management team and stay engaged with the business at a strategic level. A tax-effective approach is to use an employee stock ownership program (ESOP), which we will discuss in more detail later.

KEY IDEAS

- A Buyable Business is an asset that others want to have and are willing to pay to obtain, without you having to become their employee. You need to build your business into a Buyable Business—even if you never intend to sell it—so that you have good options if you are called elsewhere, face an emergency, or want or need to dial back your efforts.
- The default position for any business is unbuyability. You have to be intentional about building buyability into your company. Most businesses are started by technicians who initially focus on personally delivering services rather than on building a company. Being strategic and proactive helps you set up your business in a way that yields optimal outcomes.
- Reactive business owners struggle with stop–go businesses that they run on adrenaline from crisis to crisis. This kind of fuel works for a while but is not sustainable and can make owners sick or burned out

in the long term. Lack of focus on the right business model can also trap an owner into a debt spiral, eroding the value of the business. Partnership dysfunction can also force a business owner to exit the company prematurely or see it decline.

- Proactive business owners build Buyable Businesses that allow them to exit and pursue their passions, start another business with bigger potential, arrange a successful family transition, or continue at the helm of a prospering organization run by a succession management team.

TOOL FOR THE CHAPTER

Assess the buyability of your business at: BuyabilityAssessment.com

2

YOUR IDEAL LIFE

We are haunted by an ideal life, because we have within us the beginning and the possibility of it.

—PHILLIPS BROOKS

By the age of 40, Bill Gates had become the richest man on earth, according to the 1995 Forbes listing of the wealthiest people.[8] After founding Microsoft with his friend Paul Allen in 1975, Gates took it public with its IPO on March 13, 1986, when he was only 31 years old.[9] By September 1998, Gates had turned Microsoft into the world's most valuable company.

Upon reaching that summit, Gates raised his sights again. In 2000, he replaced himself at the helm by appointing Steve Ballmer to succeed him as CEO of Microsoft.[10] He then took on the role of Chief Software Architect of the company until he left this position in 2008 to dedicate his energies full-time to his charitable mission at the Bill and Melinda Gates Foundation.

Having granted $35.8 billion, Bill Gates stands as the largest donor in the world, and according to a 2017 *Guardian* article, the Gates Foundation has helped save at least 122 million lives to date.[11] Gates built the second-largest charitable foundation on Earth by attracting contributions from some of the richest entrepreneurs on the planet, including Warren Buffett, Michael Bloomberg, George Soros, and Mark Zuckerberg.[12]

But charitable work must have distracted Gates because in 2003 he relinquished the title of founder of the largest company and in 2009 he was replaced as the richest person in the world.[13] However, only temporarily. By 2018, Microsoft was back in the lead, and in April 2019, it reached over $1 trillion in market capitalization, ahead of Amazon and Google, and Gates has again overtaken Jeff Bezos on the rich list.[14]

I hope you don't think for a moment that Bill Gates keeps coming out on top by accident. He is the visionary of visionaries, a businessperson who sets out to reach the summit and hits it every time. He starts with the end in mind and doesn't stop until he attains his goals.

You may not build the biggest company or become the richest person, and you may not want to. But if you desire to build a Buyable Business, you can follow a process similar to Gates's.

In this chapter, I will show you how you can use your business as a vehicle to transport you to your ultimate purpose and lifestyle.

WHAT WOULD FULFILL YOU?

Building a Buyable Business is relatively simple, but it isn't easy. You must change how you operate, which requires stepping out of your comfort zone. But why should you make yourself uncomfortable without having a compelling reason to do so?

This is where articulating the future and Your Ideal Life come in.

Ask yourself: How would I be spending my waking hours if I could choose to do anything I wanted? Where would I be living? What would my purpose be? Who and what kind of people would I surround myself with? What would my health look like? What activities, and in which proportions, would give me the greatest satisfaction?

The reason our family moved to America was that my wife, Dora, and I could no longer visualize ourselves able to live our personal purposes in Hungary, the way we wanted.

In Budapest I had a business that I loved and that challenged me for its first eight years. But in 2010, the environment changed. More precisely, after 20 years of progress my mother country stopped moving forward and began reverting back to its long-term historical trajectory: Its post–

Berlin Wall, Western democratic evolution stalled, and provincial, feudal-istic, and nationalistic political and social structures reemerged. I could no longer believe in my original vision of building a regional M&A "power-house" from Hungary.

My dream presupposed an open society and a free market economy that continued to integrate with the Eurozone area, and where entrepreneurs would share in increasing prosperity in line with their respective economic contributions. But I could no longer rely on a fair legal system to protect my business and my family, and I couldn't live with the thought that we might have to serve an elite against our personal values, should disturbing trends continue. Dora felt similarly.

I was 45 years old at the time of our move to Virginia, and I yearned to realize our version of the American Dream, which we could no longer hope to capture in Hungary.

We knew that reinventing a career would be challenging across the At-lantic, but we believed we could be successful in a meritocratic society. I wanted to continue serving small business entrepreneurs and to remain one myself. We visualized our children getting the best education and fol-lowing their own positive purposes, and I am delighted to see them thrive here. Dora wanted to continue her professional career. We wanted to be surrounded by positive-thinking, community-minded people and operate in a trusting, informal business environment. We have been blessed with all that and more. The American Dream is alive and well.

And with all this waiting for us, I was more than willing to reach be-yond my current level of comfort in running MB Partners from across the Atlantic and to turn it into a Buyable Business.

MEANINGFUL "RETIREMENTS"

So, what would you do with your life if money was no object and you could do what you pleased? You don't have to retire to idleness, which is probably a bad idea for most people anyway, because without purposeful challenges, life offers little value. So, what would you feel fulfilled doing? Here are a few examples of meaningful post-exit futures.

Playing for Keeps: Richard Branson

Richard Branson, the flamboyant British entrepreneur and explorer, is not a seller. His Virgin Group and most of its four hundred subsidiaries are highly buyable companies, but Branson is an entrepreneur for life who doesn't seem interested in retirement. One of his talents is finding the right people to run his businesses, and he is free to contribute as much as pleases him. He enjoys tennis and vacationing with Barack Obama and other celebrities, but he gets involved in his businesses from time to time whenever something piques his interest.

Invest in Your Passion: Charles Saatchi

Charles Saatchi's compelling future was art collection. Born in 1943 to an Iraqi Jewish family in Baghdad, he and brother Maurice founded the Saatchi & Saatchi ad agency, which by 1986 had grown through acquisitions to be the largest agency in the world. In 1995, the brothers left to found another agency, M&C Saatchi, which itself grew into a global network of 66 offices. In 2007, Charles sold his stake and devoted his energies to the Saatchi Gallery of Contemporary Art. In 2010, he announced the donation of his gallery, which hosts 1.5 million visitors a year and boasts a collection valued at £37 million worth of art, to the British public.[15]

Keep Creating Businesses: Linda Nash

Linda Nash is a serial entrepreneur based in Richmond, Virginia. She started the first exclusively school-age childcare program in Richmond in 1983, which she grew to six locations, ran for 15 years, and then sold to a strategic buyer. She then designed and started the Compass Schools, a private preschool and kindergarten, where she served as CEO and board chair for three years. In 2003, Nash opened the doors to PartnerMD, a concierge practice that gives patients round-the-clock access to their doctors. She sold PartnerMD to Markel Ventures in 2011 and continued to grow the company to nine thousand members. Nash left PartnerMD in 2015 to launch another, higher-end concierge medical business called WellcomeMD, which is also close to leaving the nest. There's no telling what she will do next.[16]

Take a Break: Solt

Solt is a construction entrepreneur who builds electrical contracting businesses. He founded Epsillon in Pécs, Hungary, which he grew to $35 million in sales, with 15 percent net profit and market leadership. In 2006, we helped him sell the business to Dutch construction group Janzzen. Solt and his wife used some of the proceeds of the sale to travel extensively and educate their children in the UK. But when Solt's noncompete expired, he returned to Pécs and started another electrical contracting company because construction entrepreneurship remained his passion.

Spread Your Wisdom: Jack Welch

Jack Welch was one of the most successful CEOs of all time. He increased the market cap of General Electric from $12 billion to $410 billion during his 20 years at the helm. In 2001, he retired from GE, receiving the highest ever severance package, worth $417 million, but he didn't stop working. In 2005, he published *Winning*, a *New York Times* best-selling autobiography, and began to advise private equity firms and CEOs, became a sought-after public speaker, and cowrote a popular syndicated column for *Businessweek* with his wife, Suzy. Welch passed away in early 2020 at 84.[17]

There are many ways to be happy and fulfilled after selling a business, but the sale itself is unlikely to be the thing that makes you happy. After letting go of your company, you may feel safer and less stressed, but you will lose some status, personal connections, and the feeling of being needed and important. Your identity may also evolve as your focus shifts from building your business to other life endeavors.

The key is to know thyself. If you are clear on what you want to do outside the business you are selling, and have thought deeply about your chances of finding an equivalent or greater meaning in that pursuit, then go full steam ahead. But don't let the allure of riches paper over your deeper feelings.

THE QUESTIONS TO ASK YOURSELF

Before you embark on building a Buyable Business, consider your ideal future and specifically your answers to the following questions. Knowing how you feel about your life's Next Chapter is the first step in making it happen.

Is running the business Your Ideal Life?

Building and running a growing, prospering company can be a fulfilling and stimulating purpose. You may have already found your calling in being an entrepreneur, and if so, that is wonderful.

Running a business can be an empowering and exhilarating experience, but it is often stressful. Not just when the business is failing but also when it is prospering and manifesting growing pains.

One of the fastest-growing companies in my current hometown of Richmond, Virginia, experienced severe growing pains two years ago, which led to management changes and a more conservative strategy focused on process, cash flow, and technological improvements. The owner was delighted with the fast growth until he started running out of cash. He went through a challenging time and had to downsize the company and slow growth considerably in order to survive.

Are you ready to handle the stress of a business, especially when you own it and are exposed to the risks and costs of fixing problems?

If it's the business you want, what is your ideal role and setup in it?

Do you enjoy running the day-to-day operations of the company? Or would you prefer being a visionary leader who focuses on strategy, culture, big relationships, and acquisitions while delegating someone else to run the business for you? Or do you see yourself in a technical role inside the business?

In 2010, Bill Gates moved into the role of Chief Software Architect after appointing Steve Ballmer as CEO, although Gates remained chairman of the business until 2014.[9]

In 1983, Steve Jobs stepped down as CEO after he wooed John Sculley, who was president of PepsiCo, to become Apple's vice president and general manager of the Macintosh department. (In 1985, Jobs was pushed out by Sculley in a boardroom coup.)[18]

More recently, the founders of Google, Larry Page and Sergey Brin, stepped down from running the business in favor of focusing on their pet projects, including self-driving cars and life extension research.

There are positive and negative examples of role and setup, and it is up to you as the founder to decide and shape your future in your business as long as you control it, and potentially beyond, through a contract with the future ownership.

If Your Ideal Life is outside the business, what will sustain your satisfaction after an exit?

This is the most critical question for you to answer. As long as you control the business, you can always change your mind about your future role in it. But after the sale, there is no turning back (with rare exceptions that you will not be in control of). I had several clients who ended up regretting selling their company after they realized it had been the primary source of meaning in their lives.

Personally, I struggled with the loss of identity after selling MB Partners in 2013. Getting a financial deal and a home for my team were gratifying, but I suffered the loss of social connections and the status conferred by owning a well-known advisory business in my native land.

One of my clients, János Gréczi (more on him later), hesitated at the eleventh hour. He had to decide whether to pull the plug on the sale of his business and downsize his activities to real estate development.

I have seen successful post-business careers include running for office, becoming a best-selling author, owning or presiding over a sports team or national organization, sitting on boards, becoming a business angel or real estate investor, taking on challenging personal adventures, and…starting a new company.

Rarely did I see examples of extended vacations, golfing, boating, retiring to an exotic island, or spending full-time with grandchildren work out for ex-entrepreneurs beyond a three- to six-month period.

Your Ideal Life Questionnaire

Answering these questions will help you articulate the compelling future that is waiting to be achieved as the Next Chapter in your life:

- Is your compelling future in the business or outside of it?
- What does your role look like if your ideal future is inside the business?
- What does Your Ideal Life look like outside of your current business?
- When do you want to achieve this future?
- What will it take for you to achieve this ideal state?
- How much capital do you need to accumulate to transition to this state?

Now that you know what Your Ideal Life will look like, your next question is: What will it cost to get there? To figure this out, you have to calculate your Magic Number.

WHAT IS YOUR MAGIC NUMBER?

Do you know what a Magic Number is?

My favorite definition is from Lee Eisenberg, the former editor of *Esquire*, who said, "It is a free pass to a great life, without financial stress."[19]

Does a Magic Number sound interesting to you? Do you know yours?

When I discuss this subject with business owner and CEO peer groups, I find that only about 30 percent of entrepreneurs have a clear financial goal line. Most ignore the idea, pretending that they are doing well enough and that everything will work out for the best.

Don't delude yourself. As Yogi Berra said, "You've got to be very careful if you don't know where you are going, because you might not get there."

Remember the case of Struktoor, where the owners, Sasha and Ace, didn't know their Magic Number? They just wanted to sell their business for as much as possible and kept moving the goalpost. They got too greedy and missed their window of opportunity. The following year, the financial crisis affected the economy and softened Struktoor's numbers. By 2010, a new government had come into power, and Struktoor fell out of favor on public projects. From that point, it took only a year for the company to go under. The founders lost tens of millions of dollars and almost ended up in jail, all because they didn't know their Magic Number.

Money isn't the answer to your happiness, but envisioning the kind of life you want and what amount of money it will take for you to get there is essential. It is worth knowing up until which point money is the aim and after which point you can focus on something beyond financial wealth, something that improves your relationships, draws you forward as an inspiring purpose, builds your legacy, or does all these things. For example, Csaba was passionate about elevating the Hungarian ice hockey team, and in the process of pursuing his passion, he built a much larger legacy than he had with his company, Gulliver. Ice hockey and how the national team plays touch millions of people.

Even if you want to keep your business forever, you still need to know how much money it should make for you to pay for your ideal retirement lifestyle, you and your partner's healthcare, your hobbies, your grandchildren's education, and your charitable goals. You must build and run the business so you can harvest these amounts over the time horizon you've chosen or through a partial sale or other liquidity event.

The Magic Number Formula

If you don't know your Magic Number, don't despair. I will help you figure it out with the following exercise.

Your Magic Number depends on these variables:

- Your Annual Retirement Burn Rate
- Your desired possessions
- Your giving goals
- Your Magic Number multiple

You can determine your number in three steps.

The first step is to invoke the ideal life that *you* want to live. We're calling this your "Next Chapter." Your Next Chapter may be your retirement, or it may be your next business, charitable foundation, sports team to buy, or any other purpose that compels you to act.

Step 1: Describe Your Ideal Life

Where are you going to live? What are you going to do? Who are you taking with you on this journey? Which toys do you want to own? What does your lifestyle look like? Will you have multiple homes? Will you be supporting your family or a cause? Will you have hobbies?

Step 2: Calculate Your Annual Retirement Burn Rate

With the picture of your Next Chapter in mind, let's figure out your cost of living. Think about how much you will want to spend on the following items in your Next Chapter. For some, this may be living for simple pastimes from the age of 75. For others, it may be an adventure- or luxury-filled lifestyle from the age of 50, when perhaps some of your kids are still on your "payroll."

Use the VERIFY acronym shown in Figure 2.1 to calculate the overhead of your desired lifestyle after your Next Chapter date. In this, my personal example, I envisage a comfortable life with my wife that includes lots of travel and commuting between two homes, with my Next Chapter starting when I am in my seventies and Dora is in her mid-sixties. For us, $200,000 per year would be more than sufficient to cover our living expenses in current dollars.

Figure 2.1 Annual Retirement Burn Rate Example

Annual Retirement Burn Rate (VERIFY)	$000
Vacations, travel, memberships	50
Entertainment, gifts to self/others	60
Rent/mortgage/utilities/maintenance	30
Insurance (health, car, property, etc.)	20
Food, car expenses, household goods	40
Your Total Annual Spending	**200**

Step 3: Calculate Your Magic Number

The next step is to multiply the Annual Retirement Burn Rate by the number of years you expect to be retired. (See Figure 2.2.) According to the Social Security Administration, the average life expectancy of people who turn 65 in 2020 is just over 20 years.

The rule of thumb in the wealth management industry is that you should save 10 to 12 times your annual household income for retirement. This number assumes that your investments will grow in retirement and your lifestyle expenses will fall as time passes.

More conservatively, you might calculate your multiplier by subtracting the age at which you plan to retire from age 85 years. If you feel that you would live much longer, increase the multiplier by the number of extra years you want to give yourself beyond 85.

This life expectancy number may change with the rapidly advancing science of life extension, and some, including Dan Sullivan, founder of Strategic Coach, are preparing to live to the year 2100, when he would turn 156 years old.[20]

I plan to live to the age of 90, and I assume that my spouse will survive me by 10 years, i.e. to my 100th birthday. Therefore, as I plan to retire at 70, I would use a multiplier of 30, conservatively predicting that our nest egg would not earn a real return, but it would maintain its value during our combined 30 years of retirement.

Figure 2.2 Magic Number Calculator

Annual Retirement Burn Rate (VERIFY)	$	$
Vacations, travel, memberships	50,000	
Entertainment, gifts to self/others	60,000	
Rent/mortgage/utilities/maintenance	30,000	
Insurance (health, car, property, etc.)	20,000	
Food, car expenses, household goods	40,000	
Your Total Annual Spending (A)		**200,000**
Calculate Your Retirement Nest-Egg (A × 30) = (B)		**6,000,000**
Desired Possessions (C)		1,000,000
Giving Goals (children, grandchildren, charity) (D)		1,000,000
Your Magic Number (B + C + D)		**8,000,000**

Calculate your own at: MagicNumberCalculator.com.

As you can see in Figure 2.2, if we live a $200,000-a-year lifestyle for 30 years (hard to imagine not winding down over time), and we buy a condo in the Florida Keys on retirement and gift a million for our grandkids' education or to charity, my Magic Number is $8,000,000. This is the maximum we might need, and we will probably be fine with less.

Now for you, this equation may be very different. You may want to retire earlier or later, live a dearer or cheaper lifestyle, project a higher or lower life expectancy, and pursue more expensive or more modest hobbies and giving goals. Most entrepreneurs I share this exercise with learn that they need to accumulate less money than they had originally expected.

The exercise also varies between groups. When I have presented this exercise in group meetings, some teams turned competitive, and as they shared their nest egg targets with the rest of the group, Magic Numbers climbed until a 60-year-old startup solopreneur announced that his goal was to get to $50 million.

There is no point being carried away, unless you want to compete for the billionaire's club. You can live an affluent, varied, and full life with a few million dollars in the bank.

Keep Working Until You Reach Your Magic Number: Gramex

After I sold MB Partners in 2013, one of my partners, Róbert János Nagy, and I kept working on our most promising transaction outside the sale of the firm. This deal was to prepare beverage bottling company Gramex for exit. The owner, János, was a highly dynamic entrepreneur who had a Magic Number and focused on growing his business to that number with the plan of selling his business upon reaching it.

He had approached MB Partners in 2011, and we had valued his business at about 40 percent below his Magic Number. He hired us to help him groom the business (more on that in Chapter 9) so he could reach his Magic Number valuation as soon as possible.

A year later, we prepared for a sale, expecting the business to grow into János's Magic Number within the coming 12 months. It took a few months longer, but eventually he hit the number and was ready to retire to the Next Chapter of his life. More on him later.

The Richest Man at 40—What Is His Next Frontier?

As I mentioned earlier, Bill Gates set his sights on becoming the richest person on earth, and he hit that goal in 1995, when he turned 40 years old. I would be surprised if he didn't have a Magic Number for his charitable organization, too. The Bill and Melinda Gates Foundation has saved 122 million lives as of this writing, and Gates is only 65. If he stays in good health, his new Magic Number may be to save a billion people. Who knows?

Dan Kennedy's F-You Number

Small business marketing guru Dan Kennedy often speaks of his version of the Magic Number, which he calls the "F-You" number: Everyone has a number that allows them to say "F-You" to anyone who wants to prevent them from living the way they want. Your F-You number allows you to move to wherever you want in the world, be financially independent and secure, do what you love to do with the people you like to have around you, protected from meddling governments, employers, and peers.

The EOS Life®

Gino Wickman, creator of the Entrepreneurial Operating System®, talks about a similar concept he calls "The EOS Life." You are living The EOS Life when:

- *you are doing that you love to do*
- *with the people you love being with,*
- *making a huge difference,*
- *being compensated appropriately, and*
- *having time to pursue your other passions.*

Living The EOS Life is a lower bar than a Magic Number because it doesn't presuppose you to be financially independent but only prospering in a purposeful and social environment that fits your personality and values.

What's important when calculating your Magic Number is that you get clear on Your Ideal Life purpose, the state of being you ultimately want to pursue, the people you want to surround yourself with, the lifestyle and locations where you wish to live, the costs of being able to embark on and maintain your passion, the gadgets you want to own, and the gifts you want to make. Build your budget and figure out what it would cost to achieve it.

In the next chapter, we will review where your business is and where you need to take it so that it can launch you on the path to Your Ideal Life.

KEY IDEAS

- It is crucial for you to figure out how you would spend your time if you could choose to do anything you wanted. What does Your Ideal Life look like? What will be your purpose, lifestyle? Where would you live and with whom? Define your Next Chapter, whether it takes place inside or outside your business.
- Owning a successful business can be a source of identity, financial success, personal purpose, and fulfillment. You have options inside the business, or you can take a break and travel, invest in your passion, become a serial entrepreneur, give back as an author and speaker, or retire to a life of leisure. (That latter fulfills few.)
- Make exiting your business your goal only if you have set up a compelling alternative future for yourself. Figure out that future first.
- Your Magic Number represents a target to shoot for. Lack of an ultimate financial objective leads to eternal dissatisfaction because you will keep moving the goalpost. Use the Magic Number Formula to get a ballpark number that you need to achieve to activate your Next Chapter. Consider how much money you need to live, to get, and to give to calculate your number.

- You may find that you have already achieved your Magic Number or that your current business will not allow you to reach it. This is great information to know, because your goal then becomes the transition to your next opportunity at the earliest possible time.

TOOL FOR THE CHAPTER

Calculate your Magic Number at MagicNumberCalculator.com

3

THE VALUE YOU NEED TO CREATE

There are no unrealistic goals, only unrealistic deadlines.

—BRIAN TRACY

In the mid-2000s, I met with a fledgling entrepreneur, Tony, who owned ToolShop, an injection molding toolmaker for the auto industry. He was an ingenious craftsman of elaborate injection molding tools, and consequently all three major German carmakers, Audi, BMW, and Daimler, hired him. Later he expanded vertically into injection molding and became a Tier 2 supplier of auto parts and electrical machinery parts.

When we first met, ToolShop's annual revenue was around $16 million, generating about $4 million in earnings before interest, taxes, depreciation, and amortization (EBITDA). Nine years later, ToolShop's revenue had grown to over $27 million, and Tony had increased his EBITDA to more than $7 million.

As you can see in Table 3.1, over a 10-year period revenues grew by 69 percent, but EBITDA, which drives value, grew faster, by 78 percent, as a result of economies of scale.

The larger a company, the higher its valuation, or the multiple of EBITDA, investors are willing to pay for the business. ToolShop's EBITDA multiple went from 5.5 times to 6.5 times (see manufacturing company multiples in Table 3.3), giving an additional 18 percent boost to the company's value.

With growth of the business, ToolShop's EBITDA valuation multiple could expand further in the future to as much as eight times for a middle-market sale transaction and much higher still for large private equity deals and initial public offerings (IPOs).

The third value-enhancing factor was ToolShop's ability to pay down its debt. Say, for instance, you own a $500,000 house with a $400,000 mortgage. Your equity is worth only $100,000. By paying off your mortgage, you can quintuple the value of your asset. ToolShop did the same by paying off almost $7 million in debt and amassing $5 million in cash. This boosted enterprise value by another 29 percent.

Based on the above, the equity value of Tony's business grew from $15 million to more than $51 million, a 233 percent increase, 3.3 times the increase in its revenue between 2006 and 2015. By making your company bigger, better, and less indebted, you can increase its value exponentially. (I go deeper into the distinction of enterprise and equity values in the next section.)

Table 3.1 ToolShop Manufacturing Company

$ million	2006	2015	Growth/Year
Sales revenue	16.0	27.4	6.2%
EBITDA (A)	4.0	7.1	6.7%
EBITDA multiple (B)	5.5	6.5	
Enterprise value (A × B) = (C)	21.9	46.5	8.7%
Net cash / (debt) (D)	(6.7)	4.8	
Equity value (C – D)	15.2	51.2	14.4%

As you can see in Table 3.1, all Tony needed to do to create a highly valuable business was to keep growing the company above the rate of inflation, improve his profit margin slightly, and manage his working capital so he could repay ToolShop's debts. A mere 6 percent compounding annual growth and disciplined management of cash flows enabled the business to mature into a highly Buyable Business. ToolShop was acquired by a German industrial investor in 2015.

Note that Tony didn't achieve these results in a high-growth or high-tech, trendy business. He did it in a low-growth and unsexy industry and created a highly valuable asset by executing a plan with perseverance and discipline.

Growing the year-on-year value of your business by 25 percent allows you to increase the value of your business by 10 times in 10 years. This is often possible by growing revenue by a mere 15 percent per year, while gradually increasing your profit margins and paying off debt, like ToolShop did.

In the following section, we will figure out what it would take for your company to realize a similar result to Tony's. Are you ready?

1. First, we will perform a rough valuation for your business.
2. Then, we will figure out how much your business would have to grow to fulfill your financial goals.
3. Next, we consider the growth rate that your business requires to reach its target value over your time horizon.
4. Last, we consider how realistic it is for your company to achieve that growth rate and how you might have to tweak your plan to get to your destination. In rare cases, it may turn out that your aim is altogether unrealistic and you need an alternative plan.

VALUING YOUR PRESENT AND YOUR FUTURE

Enterprise Value versus Equity Value

We will calculate two types of value. One for valuing the business on the basis of its expected future cash flows, irrespective of the financing of the business: enterprise value. The second for valuing the shares you own in the business debt free: equity value. (See Figure 3.2.)

Recall from the ToolShop example, enterprise value, calculated as a multiple of EBITDA, grew by 8.7 percent per year, while equity value increased by a whopping 14.4 percent over the nine-year period we examined. How could that be?

When we value a company free of financial debt with negligible cash in the bank, its enterprise value and equity value are the same. It's like a house without a mortgage but with an empty money safe in it. If you own 100 percent of a $500,000 house with no debt, then this house has $500,000 of equity in it. Enterprise Value = Equity Value.

Figure 3.2 How to Calculate Equity Value

1. EBITDA × EBITDA Multiple = **Enterprise Value**
2. Enterprise Value - Debt = **Equity Value**

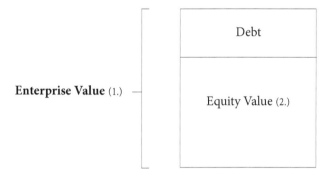

EBITDA = Earnings Before Interest, Tax, Depreciation & Amortization
EBITDA Multiple: See Table 3.3
Debt: Interest Bearing (bank loans, bonds, notes, leasing, factoring, etc.)

Equity value is what's left after selling your business and "paying off your mortgage"

However, when a company has more debt than cash, its equity value is lower than its enterprise value. And the reverse: If it has more cash than debt, then its equity value is higher than its enterprise value.

In the example, ToolShop started its nine-year run with a net debt balance of $6.7 million and ended up with net cash in its balance sheet of $4.8 million. (See Table 3.1.) The increase in its financial position created an additional $11.5 million in equity value for Tony, over and above the company's enterprise value.

So, why should you worry about these technicalities?

The enterprise/equity value distinction curiously escapes many entrepreneurs. As a result, they often neglect managing their cash, run into debt, and sometimes end up building huge, but worthless companies.

Let's now look at the most common ways investors and buyers value private businesses.

Ways to Value a Business

There are two principal approaches to valuing a business. You can either look at it as the sum of the value of its assets, or you can base the valuation on the business's future expected cash earnings. Use one or the other method, but never both together.

Because the reason a business exists is to add value, most businesses should be worth more based on their future expected earnings than on an asset basis. Therefore, in most cases, earnings valuations should be used.

However, when the entrepreneur doesn't create additional value (which we call "goodwill") by combining these assets, the business will be worth only the sum of its components. In such cases, asset valuations should be used.

Earnings-Based Valuation Methods

Because most viable businesses have some goodwill value in addition to the value of their assets, we will focus on earnings-based valuations.

So, how do you value small and midsized businesses on an earnings basis? You calculate earnings-based valuations using projected future cash flows or, with a simplified approach, using earnings multiples.

Owner's Discretionary Earnings Multiples

Companies with earnings of less than $1 million are typically mom-and-pop, owner-managed businesses. For these, the limiting factor is the management, which will leave the business with the sale and which typically cannot be replaced by competent hired hands at a cost the business can afford. These businesses need another owner-manager who will invest time and energy as well as capital. The price of such a business is one to three times the seller's annual discretionary earnings (SDE). The SDE is all the money that the owner can harvest per year from the business, both as an employee and as an entrepreneur.

EBITDA Multiples

Companies that make roughly a $1 million or more cash profit per annum are considered to be semi-independent from their owners or sometimes even self-managing. Here the value-limiting factor no longer is the management but instead is sustainable cash profitability. Therefore, these companies are valued at a multiple of profit. Profit may be defined as profit before tax, EBITDA or adjusted EBITDA.

EBITDA is an interesting metric. It was coined by John Malone, the "Cable King," who consolidated cable companies in the 1970s, and EBITDA was popularized by leverage buyout investors, such as KKR, in the 1980s.

EBITDA's appeal is that it is a simple proxy for cash flow that can be computed by looking at an income statement, without having to rely on supplementary financial records, which are often unavailable or inaccurate for smaller businesses. The weakness of EBITDA is that it ignores changes in working capital, which can be a major cash outflow for growing companies, as well as capital expenditures necessary to replace broken-down assets or to invest in expansion.

EBITDA is useful for turnaround investors who aren't worried about capital investments and for banks that want to know how much money they can get their hands on from the company if it were to default. Because banks love the measure, buyout investors began using it to calculate how much they could afford to pay for companies over and above the borrowing capacity of their acquisition target.

Banks expressed this debt capacity as the multiple of EBITDA they were willing to lend to a company. Later, buyout firms started using that same measure to determine how much they were prepared to invest. For example, a midsized cable company may have a debt capacity of 3.5 times

EBITDA, and a private equity buyer may achieve its target return while investing a maximum of three times EBITDA. This would give the cable company an enterprise value of 6.5 times EBITDA.

Adjusted EBITDA takes into account the fact that most small businesses are not fully transparent and some personal or inessential expenses may flow through their income statements. These expenses are added back to EBITDA as adjustments to show the true income-producing capacity of the business. Any excess salary an independent manager would have to be paid to replace the seller represents a negative adjustment to the EBITDA.

Other Valuation Methods

Some investors, especially in capital-intensive industries, use **EBIT multiples** to avoid overstating earnings. EBIT, earnings before interest and taxes, calculates profit after depreciation expenses, assuming that these would have to be plowed back into capital investments to maintain the production assets of the company.

Professional investors also study a handful of closely **comparable transactions** to gain deeper insight into valuation factors. Examining the valuations of publicly listed companies can also provide clues. Private transaction data is not available in the United States, but in some European countries these details are reported to authorities and can be researched, and they are aggregated by information providers such as Bureau van Dijk. These European multiples are worth studying because they approximate the valuations of US companies.

Projecting future cash flows can be a robust approach, but these valuations are highly sensitive to assumptions, such as assumptions of future economic growth and required rates of return. They need to be sanity-checked using multiples and asset-based methods.

The bigger and more sophisticated a company, the more approaches investors will use to understand the business and its potential from many angles.

For its simplicity, ubiquity, and the general availability of benchmarks, we will use EBITDA multiples in this book. A fairly reliable and freely available tool is the Pepperdine Graziadio Business School's annual Private Capital Markets Report, which segments valuation data by ten major industries and sizes of EBITDA.[21] (See Table 3.3.)

As you can see from the figures below, the larger the business, the higher the multiple. This is because bigger companies are more stable and bigger transactions are more profitable for investors. Stable and more profitable investments attract more demand, which in turn drives up prices.

Furthermore, bigger companies tend to have more market power, are less dependent on their management, can afford to pay for new management, and have the muscle to restructure if they are underperforming. Smaller companies are harder to fix.

Table 3.3 Median Deal Multiples by EBITDA Size

Sector/EBITDA	≤ $0.99M	$1–4.99M	$5–9.99M	$10–24.99M	$25–49.99M	≤ $.50M
Manufacturing	5.0	5.5	6.5	7.5	7.5	8.0
Construction & Engineering	3.5	4.5	5.0	6.5	9.0	n/a
Consumer Goods & Services	4.3	5.5	5.8	6.5	8.0	8.0
Wholesale & Distribution	5.5	5.5	5.8	7.5	7.5	n/a
Business Services	3.0	4.8	5.3	6.0	7.0	7.0
Basic Materials & Energy	5.0	5.5	6.0	6.0	6.5	7.0
Health Care & Biotech	4.3	5.5	7.3	7.5	8.0	10.0
IT	7.0	7.5	8.0	8.5	9.0	10.0
Financial Services	5.5	6.0	7.5	7.8	8.0	8.0
Media & Entertainment	4.0	5.5	6.0	6.5	8.3	n/a

Source: *Pepperdine Equity Research Report 2019*, Private Capital Markets Project, Graziadio Business School, https://bschool.pepperdine.edu/institutes-centers/centers/applied-research/research/pcmsurvey.

The business that was worth nothing

In the mid-2000s, I received a call from Roland and Seph, two entrepreneurs whose business wholesaled Chinese-made home goods. At the time, their business, Exdom, made annual sales of about $12 million, with $2 million of EBITDA. We looked at the valuation tables and concluded that the business was worth about $8 million on a cash and debt-free (enterprise value) basis.

Our preliminary valuation excited Roland and Seph, who wanted to engage us to find a buyer for their business. However, after poring over Exdom's balance sheet, we discovered that an $8 million fully drawn credit line financed the business. The bank loans funded inventories and receivables worth nine months of sales and receivables from big-box stores, which took two to three months to pay their bills after taking delivery. Exdom's working capital need was standard in its industry, and the owners could not reduce it without losing their customers to the competition.

So, the company was valued at $8 million without debt, and after paying off its $8 million debt it was worth $0 to its shareholders. The value of the mortgage equaled the value of the house.

Roland and Seph were crushed to realize that their shares were worth practically nothing and they wondered how to move forward. On top of having no equity value, Exdom faced the risk of going down should any of its major customers became insolvent.

We suggested that Roland and Seph wind down Exdom. Over the following months, they sold out their inventories and collected all receivables, which allowed them to repay bank loans. They let go of employees and leased the company's warehouse. In the following years, they paid off the mortgage and milked the real estate for passive income.

Now let's see what your business is worth based on its EBITDA.

VISUALIZE THE GAP

The Current Equity Value of Your Business

Follow these steps to determine the equity value of your business:

1. Find your company's latest full-year EBITDA. You may use your expected year-end EBITDA if you are getting close to the end of the year.
2. Multiply your EBITBA with the EBITDA multiple from Table 3.3 that pertains to your industry and your business size (measured by the size range of your EBITDA).
3. From the product arrived at in step two deduct the total outstanding interest-bearing debt that finances your business.

For example, here is a business services firm that has current EBITDA of $1.5 million and outstanding interest-bearing debt of $2 million.

Current Equity Value = (EBITDA × EBITDA multiple) – Debt

Therefore, the Current Equity Value is: ($1.5 million × 4.8) – $2.0 million = $5.2 million.

Now let's look at what value you need to grow your business to in order to harvest your Magic Number. I call this Target Equity Value.

The Target Equity Value of Your Business

You can determine the target value of your business by using EBITDA multiples typical in your industry for a company of your size. According to the Pepperdine report, 60 percent of businesses are principally valued based on EBITDA and adjusted EBITDA multiples. (See Figure 3.4.)

Figure 3.4 The Popularity of Different Valuation Methods

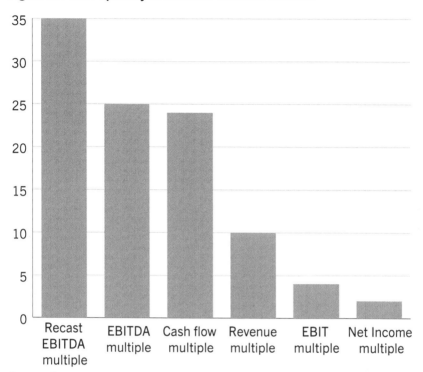

Source: *Pepperdine Equity Research Report 2019*, Private Capital Markets Project, Graziadio Business School, https://bschool.pepperdine.edu/institutes-centers/centers/applied-research/research/pcmsurvey.

By multiplying the EBITDA profit of your business with the relevant EBITDA multiple from Table 3.3, you can calculate the enterprise value of your business. The enterprise value of your company less any interest-bearing debt plus any cash in the balance sheet yields the equity value of your business. This is the value that your business's shareholders share on the basis of their respective equity stakes in the company.

Using your Magic Number and percentage equity stake, you can then reverse-engineer the size that your company must grow to in order to yield your Magic Number after capital gains taxes. The time horizon is your expected date of retirement or the date of your planned cashing out from your current business. (See Figure 3.5.)

Figure 3.5 Target Equity Value Calculation Example

Your Magic Number (A)	$8m
Your Net Worth outside the business (B)	($2m)
Amount You Need from Business for Next Chapter (A – B) = (C)	$6m
% of Equity You Own in the Business (D)	58%
Capital Gains Tax + Local Taxes on Exit (E)	26%
$ Paid for Your Stake (Purchase Price or Investment) (F)	$1m

Target Equity Value = [C + (C – F) × E] / D
= [$6m + ($6m - $1m) × 26%] / 58% = **$12.6m**

In this example, if your Magic Number is $8 million, and you have a net worth of $2 million outside the business, then you have to harvest another $6 million from your company. Assuming you have a 58 percent equity stake in the business, were liable to pay 20 percent federal capital gains tax (CGT) and 6 percent state CGT, the enterprise value of your business would have to grow to $12.6 million to yield the $6 million in equity value that is missing from your Magic Number.

Now calculate at what annual percentage rate you need to grow the value of your business over your time horizon (n). (See Figure 3.6.)

Figure 3.6 The Growth You Need: Compound Annual Growth Rate (CAGR)

The CAGR You Need = (Target Equity Value $ / Current Equity Value $) $^{1/n}$ – 1

Example: Target Equity Value = $12.6m
Current Equity Value = $5.2m
Years to Exit (n) = 5 years

The CAGR You Need = (12.6 / 5.2)$^{1/5}$ – 1 = **19.4%**

The Target EquityValue is $12.6 million, the Current Equity Value is $5.2 million, and your time horizon to exit (n) is five years. The value growth percentage per annum required can be calculated using the following equation:

(Target Equity Value ÷ Current Equity Value)$^{1/n}$ – 1

The percentage the business must grow per year in the current example is ($12.6 million ÷ $5.2 million)$^{1/5}$ − 1 = 19.4%.

Is it too aggressive to expect to grow the value of a business by 19.4 percent a year? According to the 2019 Pepperdine Capital Markets report, small cap private equity funds expect 20 percent to 30 percent annual returns from their portfolio companies.

In the earlier example, ToolShop grew its value by 14.4 percent per annum over a nine-year period by increasing sales at less than half this rate, at 6.2 percent. The rest of ToolShop's annual growth in equity value came from improving its EBITDA margin (0.5% increase), expanding its EBITDA multiple (2.0%), and paying off financial debt (5.7%). Corresponding improvements for the company in this example would reduce the required top-line growth to around 11.6 percent.

The 11.6 percent annual revenue growth requirement compares favorably with what private equity investors expect from similar size investments. Based on a 2019 survey by the Graziadio Business School of Pepperdine University, equity investors in small to medium companies expect 17 percent revenue growth and 16 percent EBITDA growth from their investee companies.[22] (See Figure 3.7.)

Figure 3.7 Minimum and Expected Annual Growth Rates for Investee Companies

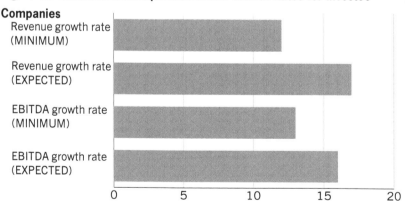

Source: *Pepperdine Equity Research Report 2019*, Private Capital Markets Project, Graziadio Business School, https://bschool.pepperdine.edu/institutes-centers/

centers/applied-research/research/pcmsurvey.

In 2019, my clients who were implementing EOS averaged 22.1 percent revenue growth and 27.5 percent profit growth. According to Vistage International, the largest CEO coaching organization in the United States, its member companies grew revenues on average by 28 percent in 2017.[23] On the basis of these figures, 19.4 percent annual growth looks reasonable.

If you feel 19.4 percent growth is too aggressive, you could give yourself more time to get there. In the example, if we extend the time horizon to exit by two years, to seven years, the annual required growth rate in equity value drops to 13.5 percent.

With that, you have designed your personal future and clarified what it will take for you to get there. In Part Two, I will show you how to orchestrate your business so that it starts progressing toward achieving your objectives.

KEY IDEAS

- Determine where you are and where you must get to over a specific time horizon in terms of the value of your stake in your business. If the necessary annual value increase is reasonable, you have a plan.
- Assuming your business is beyond the mom-and-pop stage and is at least partially self-managed, you can value it using EBITDA multiples by industry and size of business. The value of your equity is your business' latest EBITDA, multiplied by the EBITDA multiple, less your company's average annual financial debt. Beware of growth fueled by borrowing because it can diminish the value of your business.
- As you increase the size of your business, gain economies of scale, and pay down debt, the value of your business will increase faster than your top line. ToolShop grew its revenue by only 6 percent per annum, but its equity value compounded by 14 percent per year over the same period, tripling ToolShop's equity value in 10 years. A year-on-year value growth of 25 percent for 10 years would increase the value of your business by 10 times.

- If the required growth rate to reach your Next Chapter financial goals is still too high, you may have to commit to working in the business longer or to using the current business as a springboard to a more promising entrepreneurial venture, as an intermediate step toward achieving Your Ideal Life.
- If you find that your equity stake is worth more already than your Magic Number, then it is time to reevaluate whether you are living Your Ideal Life already, or you're ready to make a near-term change.

TOOL FOR THE CHAPTER

Explore the value of your business, and the growth you need from it to harvest your Magic Number, at ValueAndGrowthCalculator.com

PART TWO:
ORCHESTRATE
YOUR BUSINESS

*When you build systems, they can help you orchestrate,
and orchestration helps you create the habits that continuously improve the systems*

—MICHAEL GERBER, "BUILDING SYSTEMS THAT REPLACE YOU"

In Part One, we designed Your Ideal Life and gained clarity on where you want to go, by when, and what it will take to get there. In Part Two, we will dive into your first steps forward, namely, to orchestrate your business using time-tested management concepts.

We start by reviewing the context of The Seven Management Concepts that have emerged over the past hundred years or so, how they came about, and why they are important. Then we will examine 10 of the most prominent Management Blueprints so that you can understand them and begin to see whether integrating some or all of these concepts into your business will advance your enterprise toward your target value. Finally, I will guide you through examples of how some of these Management Blueprints implement the Seven Management Concepts.

Leveraging time-tested management concepts in your business in the process of creating a Buyable Business is like picking the low-hanging fruit.

(4)

THE SEVEN MANAGEMENT CONCEPTS

*Your first and foremost job as a leader is to take charge
of your own energy and then to help orchestrate the
energy of those around you.*

—PETER F. DRUCKER

In 2005, I read Michael Gerber's *E-Myth* and was instantly smitten. He talks about a recipe for building scalable businesses, and he uses McDonald's as an example. When you buy a McDonald's franchise, you get a complete, proven system and you just have to follow the recipe to be successful.

This sounded like a magical concept to me. A proven system to make a business successful, one that eliminates all the false starts and guesswork.

I spent the next two months figuring out all the elements of *E-Myth* so that I could implement them at MB Partners. I thought some parts were still missing, so I bought *E-Myth Mastery*, a 430-page tome, and underlined and made notes on each chapter, trying to reconstruct the recipe. Next, I implemented each chapter as best I could in my M&A consulting business.

Much of it worked, and I ignored the parts that did not. I was so excited by this system that I started a side business called *Systemize* and pitched other entrepreneurs on making their businesses self-managing. My side business eventually ran out of steam and we had to close it down. But MB Partners had a glorious run on the back of *E-Myth*. By 2007, we led the market in Hungary, ahead of our 500-pound gorilla competitor, Deloitte. That was a sweet "victory" we had been itching to achieve since 2003.

Seven years later, when I arrived in America, I picked up a copy of Gino Wickman's *Traction*. It's another "recipe book" for building a substantial business. It, too, mesmerized me, and I introduced its most important tools to MB Partners over the next couple of months. The system worked and allowed me to delegate and remotely manage my team from Virginia. (I tell you more about what happened next later in this book.) Both *E-Myth* and *Traction* enabled me to inject structure and time-tested principles into the operation of my company. I call these principles Management Blueprints.

In Part Two of this book, we will orchestrate your business for growth. But first let's look at The Seven Management Concepts you will leverage in that process, where they come from, and why they matter.

THREE WAYS TO BUILD A BUSINESS

I believe there are three ways to approach building a business. Each is valid and a fit for a different type of entrepreneur. Let's look at each in turn.

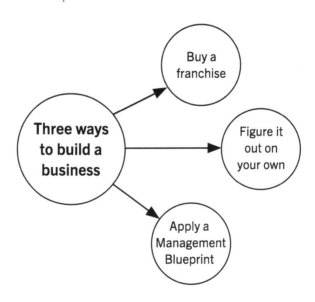

Approach One: Buy a Franchise

The first approach is the "franchise prototype way," advocated by Michael Gerber in *E-Myth*. When you buy a franchise, you get a complete blueprint for building a certain type of branded company, like a UPS Store or a Subway sandwich shop. You don't have to come up with any ideas on your own. In fact, the fewer ideas (temptations) you have to customize the system and the more rigidly you follow the recipe, the higher are your chances of success.

Trouble is, most entrepreneurs hate being micromanaged, even by a successful recipe. You embarked on running your own business to enjoy the freedom and the no-limit potential that comes with it. Following a recipe is boring. There has to be a better way, and you may feel sure you'll come up with it.

Buying a franchise has these pros and cons:

PROS:	CONS:
• Turnkey system • Proven for a specific type of business (e.g. Subway shop)	• Requires up-front investment • Economic profit skimmed by franchisor • Little room for innovation

Approach Two: Trial and Error on Your Own

Most entrepreneurs go with the second way of building a business: the trial-and-error method. This is also a "proven system," provided you don't burn through all your cash reserves before breaking even. Unfortunately, research shows that it takes 15 years to break through to outstanding success. Gene Landrum in *Entrepreneurial Genius* gives two dozen examples, from Richard Branson and Jeff Bezos to Michael Dell. They all put in their 15 years, although some of them started as young as age 14, such as Branson with *Student* magazine and Dell starting a stamp auction business at the age of twelve.[24]

The trial-and-error method works, but it takes 15 plus years to break through for the best of us, and most entrepreneurs never make it with that method.

Here are the benefits and detriments of this business-building approach:

PROS:	CONS:
• Complete creative freedom • May innovate a better mousetrap	• Typical learning curve over 15 years • 90 percent of start-ups fail within 10 years

Approach Three: Use a Management Blueprint

Fortunately, there is a third way. I call it "using a Management Blueprint." A Management Blueprint is a generic franchise system that you can implement in most companies irrespective of the industry. It is less rigid than a franchise model, allowing enough flexibility so entrepreneurs don't feel straight-jacketed.

Here are the pros and cons:

PROS:	CONS:
• Minimizes the learning curve • High rate of success • Low cost and no profit sharing	• Requires commitment and discipline • Professional help recommended

I talk more about the Management Blueprints available and the companies that can leverage each in the next chapter. Before we go there, I would like to show you the building blocks of these blueprints so you understand where they come from and why they make sense to implement in your business.

Having combed the 10 popular business blueprints on the market, I identified seven fundamental management concepts that, combined in various ways, make up these blueprints. Not all the blueprints incorporate every management concept, but they each use several, and none has come up with an eighth of comparable importance. (See Figure 4.1.)

Figure 4.1 The Seven Management Concepts

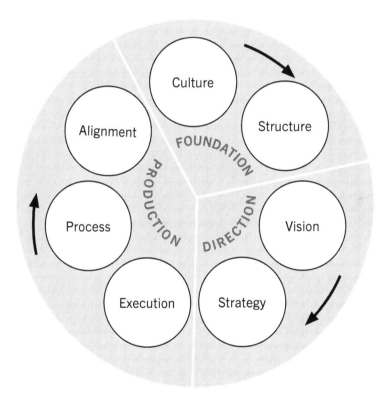

In the following pages, I introduce The Seven Management Concepts and share the stories behind each of them. I have grouped the management concepts into three categories: Foundation, Direction and Production.

CONCEPT 1: CULTURE—CHESTER BARNARD

*The responsibility of the executive is to create a sense of
purpose and moral code; to establish systems of communication;
and to ensure that people cooperate.*

—CHESTER BARNARD

To work effectively, organizations must forge individual employees into a cohesive force by creating a culture that inspires and motivates people to strive and cooperate for the common good.

Chester Barnard, the "Jack Welch of AT&T" in the 1920s and 1930s, discovered that most organizations were short-lived because they lacked effectiveness and efficiency. He defined effectiveness as the ability to accomplish stated goals, and he recognized that having unmotivated employees was highly inefficient. He concluded that for a company to last, it had to be both effective (goal driven) and efficient (have a motivated workforce).

Barnard recognized that a company is a cooperative system and its success depends on the health of the organization. Organizational health requires effective communication from a leadership aligned around a moral purpose that drives the organization. That purpose had to be relatable to employees, one with which they could align their own motivations. Such motivations might include pride in doing an excellent job, the quality of cooperation, personal development, and comfort and social relationships. Employees will accept orders from a person to the degree that the person possesses not just positional authority but also leadership authority, based on superior abilities.

Barnard also found that cohesion and self-esteem help build excellent teams. In his seminal book *The Functions of the Executive*, Barnard was the first to describe an effective company culture. This mattered, because he was one of the foremost practicing CEOs of his age.

Organizations are cooperative systems that need goal-driven and motivated employees. Building an effective company culture requires a relatable moral purpose, clearly communicated, and the opportunity for employees to pursue personal development and form positive social relationships.

CONCEPT 2: STRUCTURE —ALFRED CHANDLER

Unless structure follows strategy, inefficiency results.

—ALFRED D. CHANDLER

A clear and functional organizational structure is critical for any company to facilitate clear decision making, accountability, and communication. The first to articulate the significance of this idea was Alfred D. Chandler.

Chandler, born in 1918, was a business history professor at Harvard and Johns Hopkins Universities. He won the Pulitzer Prize for his book *The Visible Hand*, about how managerial firms developed after the rail network made mass production and mass distribution possible.

He studied the largest and most successful corporations of his age, including General Motors, DuPont, Sears Roebuck, Standard Oil of New Jersey (now Exxon), and others, to understand how they developed their organizations.

Initially, all these companies were organized with a centralized and functionally departmentalized structure, where each functional unit reported to the CEO, as shown in Figure 4.2.

Figure 4.2 Functional (U-Form) Organizational Chart

```
                              ┌──────────┐
                              │   CEO    │
                              └──────────┘
```

Vice President, Operations	Vice President, Marketing	Vice President, Finance	Vice President, Human Resources	Vice President, R & D
Plant Managers	Regional Sales Managers	Controller	Labor Relations Director	Scientific Director
Shift Supervisors	District Sales Managers	Accounting Supervisor	Plant Human Resource Manager	Lab Manager

Over time, companies expanded into multiple geographies or multiple product areas so that decision making was much more diverse and complex. This forced a switch to a divisional M-form structure, which decentralized power and lent autonomy to divisions so they could make faster decisions on the spot. (See Figure 4.3.)

Figure 4.3 Divisional (M-Form) Organizational Chart

The multidivisional structure decentralized the entrepreneurial function to divisions, which could grow using the capabilities and resources of the parent organization. Over time, this mobility increased competition as divisions of Japanese and European companies expanded into the United States.

International competition increased capacity and depressed prices, compressing profit margins. This pushed large corporations to diversify into unrelated products and services with perceived higher profit potential, triggering the age of conglomerates. The number of mergers and acquisitions tripled from 2,000 to 6,000 a year between 1961 and 1965.

However, these conglomerates ran into communications challenges between the center and the disparate operating divisions, some of which became powerful baronies, while others were oppressed by functional bureaucrats who ill understood their different divisions. The resulting weakness in management led to the mass sell-off of divisions and subsidiaries that triggered the rise of the mergers and acquisition industry.

The goal of most restructurings was to refocus on core activities where the firm had the strongest production, marketing, and research capabilities. The evolution of organizational structures turned the corner and returned to the functional form. In practice, many organizations encompass a mix of functional and divisional elements.

Entrepreneurial businesses are often haphazardly organized around personalities and personal relationships, leading to confusion, information bottlenecks, and lack of accountability. Visualizing and then defining the key functions and roles required for the organization rapidly improve delegation, communications, and management effectiveness.

CONCEPT 3: VISION—ABRAHAM MASLOW

What a man can be, he must be. This need we call self-actualization.

—ABRAHAM MASLOW

Having satisfied their basic needs, humans are then driven by curiosity and self-actualization. Companies can harness this human energy by creating an exciting vision.

Abraham Maslow, an American psychologist, was born in a Ukrainian Jewish family in Brooklyn, New York, in 1908. Being a father of two during World War II, he escaped the draft, but the horrors of war and his desire for peace led him to his groundbreaking studies in the psychology of self-actualization.

Building on Freud's work but studying healthy instead of sick individuals, he developed the field of humanistic or positive psychology. The belief that people possess the inner resources for growth and therapy, guided him. He saw his role as one of helping to remove obstacles to achieving growth. To be mentally healthy, individuals must take responsibility for their actions, and the goal of living is personal growth and understanding.

Maslow developed his famous Hierarchy of Needs with seven levels: (1) physiological, (2) safety, (3) belonging, (4) esteem, (5) cognitive, (6) aesthetic, and (7) self-actualization. (See Figure 4.4.) People satisfy lower-level needs first before paying attention to higher-level needs. Deficiencies in the lower four levels frustrate, but their fulfillment does not motivate individuals.

What drives people is fulfillment of the three high-level needs, including satiating their curiosity, developing aesthetic sensibility, and achieving self-actualization. Maslow defined self-actualization as when a person fully uses their talents and interests and becomes everything they are capable of becoming.

Figure 4.4 Maslow's Expanded Hierarchy of Needs

With the dramatic rise of income levels and the knowledge economy since World War II, substantial numbers of people have moved up Maslow's pyramid, and more people than ever are looking for fulfillment of their higher-level needs. This is especially visible in the millennial generation, members of which want to work with companies that are making a contribution to humanity.

Maslow focused attention on how important it is to harness the inner drive of future generations to achieve positive purposes. Setting a vision for your business that everyone can both emotionally and logically connect to is a critical component of building a talent-attracting and motivated workforce.

CONCEPT 4: STRATEGY — PETER DRUCKER

The best way to predict the future is to create it.

—PETER F. DRUCKER

Strategic planning allows businesses to focus their resources on the most promising opportunities and to deliberately pursue them, while releasing resources by abandoning opportunities that no longer have potential.

Born in 1909 in Vienna, Austria-Hungary, Peter F. Drucker, American author, educator, and management consultant, was possibly the most important thought leader of the world of management and the person who made business management the focus of academic research. Drucker predicted several major trends in postwar economic development, including privatization, decentralization, the rise of Japan's economic power, the importance of marketing, and the emergence of the knowledge worker and the information society. He advised the heads of General Motors, Sears, IBM, General Electric, and the American Red Cross. Drucker's 39 books appear in 36 languages.

Drucker spoke about designing the ideal business and figuring out how to create it. He suggested starting with a broad sketch and correcting and refining as you go along. The improvement in performance and results will come as the business moves with determination toward its vision.[25]

In the same book, he explains that a business must focus on three priority areas:

- Making a **big push where a great opportunity exists** to achieve extraordinary results
- **Rapidly and purposefully abandoning** what no longer holds potential to create resources for and stimulate the search for the new

- **Ignoring "also runs,"** where neither push nor abandonment holds much promise

In *The Five Most Important Questions*, Drucker lists the questions most pertinent for creating a strategic plan:

1. **What is your mission?** What are you trying to achieve, what is your organization's reason for being, what does the organization provide to society that justifies its existence?
2. **Who is your customer?** What are your customers' demographics, primary needs, physical and psychological needs, and location? Who should you be serving, who are not yet your customers, and which customers should you abandon?
3. **What does the customer value?** Which benefits, fulfilled needs, and satisfaction do customers receive nowhere else? What do these customers value about your organization? What do they want long term that you could provide? How well do you provide the value they need?
4. **What are your results?** To what extent have you achieved these results? How well are you using your human and financial resources? How effectively are you fulfilling your brand promise?
5. **What is your plan?** What have you learned? Where should you focus your efforts? What should you do differently? What is your plan to achieve results?

Answering Drucker's five penetrating questions enables you to define the direction and prioritize the resources of your organization.

CONCEPT 5: EXECUTION — ANDY GROVE

There are so many people working so hard and achieving very little.

—ANDREW S. GROVE

Strategy execution requires robust goal setting, the reframing of emotionally taxing situations, and the open and honest search for the truth, however painful.

Peter Drucker's successor as the preeminent management thinker is Andy Grove, the legendary CEO who led Intel to become the world's largest manufacturer of semiconductors. His peers and mentees called him "the guy who drove the growth phase" of Silicon Valley, and he was the one who Steve Jobs called for advice before returning to Apple in July 1997.[26]

Andy Grove started as an engineer, but he turned himself into a manager to save Intel from the fate of undermanaged Fairchild Semiconductor, which the three Intel founders, Robert Noyce, Gordon Moore of Moore's Law fame, and Andy Grove, left to strike out on their own in 1968. During Grove's tenure as CEO, Intel's market capitalization grew from $4 billion to $197 billion, making it the seventh-largest company in the world, with 64,000 employees.[27]

Grove found the time to write several acclaimed books, including the management classic *High Output Management*, which several Silicon Valley stars, including venture capitalist Ben Horowitz, consider a treasure chest of management insights.

I consider Grove the father of business execution because he gave us the following three critical management ideas:

Objectives and Key Results (OKRs)

Grove embraced and refined Peter Drucker's goal-setting approach: management by objectives. He called the approach objectives and key results, which his Intel disciple and early Google investor John Doerr shortened to "OKRs." The idea behind OKRs is that a company should set a handful of strategic objectives each quarter to rally the organization around and to ensure that people not only run the business but also keep moving it forward. Each of these objectives is measured by key results.

Grove gives this example of an OKR:[28]

Objective: [Intel] wants to dominate the midrange microcomputer component business.

Key Result for this quarter: Win 10 new designs for the 8085—it's a milestone for the above objective.

With OKRs, a company can set priorities that rally the organization, cascade these priorities down the organization, and create transparency between departments and individuals around the major initiatives everyone is pushing.

Reframing

In his other best-selling business book, *Only the Paranoid Survive*, Grove tells the story of how Intel pivoted from memory chips to microprocessors after Japanese competition eroded its advantage in the former.

In Grove's biography, Richard Tedlow tells the following story: "At one point in mid-1985, after a year of 'aimless wandering,' Grove said to Moore: 'If we got kicked out and the board brought in a new CEO, what do you think he would do?' Moore immediately replied, 'He would get us out of memories.' I stared at him, numb, and said, 'Why shouldn't you and I walk through the door, come back, and do it ourselves?'"[29]

Grove had a unique ability to distance himself emotionally from a situation he was invested in, reframe it, and make a cold-headed decision. That is strategy execution at its best.

Constructive Confrontation

Grove explains his philosophy as this: "Business success contains the seeds of its own destruction" because it breeds complacency and thus failure.[30] To avoid complacency, Grove created a no-frills egalitarian atmosphere at Intel, where even the CEO worked in a cubicle and had no reserved parking space.

He encouraged people to speak up and practice "constructive confrontation," where anyone in the company was allowed to confront him. Engineers vigorously debated ideas, with no feelings spared, a method adopted by mentees, including Steve Jobs.[31] The ideas that could survive the fierce scrutiny of a team of Intel engineers would be the best of the best, the theory goes.

As Grove told the *Chicago Tribune* in 1996: "We encourage our people to deal with problems without flinching. At its best, the method means that people deal with each other bluntly."[32]

Pat Gelsinger, a former Intel executive who later became CEO of VMware, describes sessions with Grove as dentistry without novocaine. "If you went into a meeting, you'd better have your data; you'd better have your opinion; and if you can't defend your opinion, you have no right to be there," he told Bloomberg.[33]

Execution requires a willingness to stare brutal facts in the face. In goal setting, to say no to most things to be able to do a few. In strategy, to pivot when past decisions no longer serve the business. And in debates, to share and hear painful truths to correct mistakes for the greater good of the business.

CONCEPT 6: PROCESS - FREDERICK TAYLOR

On Taylor's "scientific management" rests the tremendous surge of affluence in the last seventy-five years which has lifted the working masses in the developed countries well above any level recorded before.

—PETER F. DRUCKER

The first and oldest management concept is process design. Processes allow you to systemize your business. Whatever you can do based on decades of experience and intuition, you can delegate to less learned and skilled people using effective processes. Systemizing your business empowers your people to get more done and to be much more successful than they could be if they were to try figuring things out for themselves or emulating others.

Modern management science redesigned ad hoc work methods scientifically. The first management book ever published, *The Principles of Scientific Management*, appeared in 1911 from the pen of Frederick Winslow Taylor.

Taylor was born in 1856 into an upper-middle-class family, but his failing eyesight prompted him to turn down Harvard and instead join a Pennsylvania steel company as an apprentice. He soon recognized that his fellow laborers did all they could to limit their production under the false belief that the amount of work was fixed and that the faster they delivered, the sooner they or their coworkers would be laid off.

Taylor redesigned some work processes scientifically and persuaded his company's owner to let him pay more to those who followed his instructions. Whenever he did that, productivity skyrocketed.

Taylor was multitalented, having won in tennis doubles at the precursor to the US Open, finished fourth in golf at the 1900 Olympics, and received $100,000 for a patent in England. Financially independent, he spent his last decade promoting scientific management methods.

Taylor's scientific management comprised four principles:

1. Replace rule-of-thumb methods with scientifically designed processes.
2. Scientifically select, develop, and train employees.
3. Provide detailed instructions and supervision.
4. Divide the work between managers (planning) and workers (execution).

Taylor's influence led to the development of industrial and organizational psychology and Harvard's first MBA program, and it catalyzed the management consulting profession.

Scientific management revolutionized the running of railroads and reformed the Canadian textile industry; the French government mandated its use during World War I; and Lenin and Stalin applied Taylor's concepts to build up the Soviet manufacturing industry.

Henry Ford built on scientific management principles to develop the assembly line and a system of mass production that revolutionized industry all over the world.

Most entrepreneurial companies fail to leverage processes for increasing organization and efficiency. Instituting simple processes can kickstart delegation and teamwork and energize employees.

CONCEPT 7: ALIGNMENT — JIM COLLINS

Building a visionary company requires
1 percent vision and 99 percent alignment.

—JIM COLLINS

In two of his books, *Built to Last* (published in 1994, with Jerry Porras) and *Good to Great* (2001), business advisor Jim Collins writes extensively about how important it is to align an organization with its values and vision. Having a vision without organizational alignment is worthless. Alignment breathes value into the vision: when everyone in the company is rowing in the same direction.

Collins graduated from Stanford as a math major and later obtained an MBA. In a stint with McKinsey & Company, he was exposed to a project by Tom Peters and Robert Waterman that led to them writing an iconic business book together, *In Search of Excellence*. This may have inspired Collins to return to Stanford Business School as a researcher and professor.[34]

In his extensively researched books, Collins concludes that companies that remain highly successful over a long period of time practice alignment as a way of life. On average, it takes four years for the average "GOOD-TO-GREAT-COMPANY" to crystallize its strategy, identity, and business models, what Collins calls the "Hedgehog Concept."[35] "It was an inherently iterative process—comprising piercing questions, vigorous debate, resolute action, and autopsies without blame—a cycle repeated over and over by the right people."

After an organization's vision has been nailed down, it remains critical that all stakeholders consistently practice alignment to ensure everyone is fully in tune and excited by the vision.

Articulating and seeking alignment with an inspiring purpose and vision, business leaders can tap into their employees' emotional drivers and harness and channel an energy that most companies leave underutilized. In our electronics-distracted and values-confused age, people are starved to be part of a compelling story, which they can do by aligning themselves with a company that drives positive change.

KEY IDEAS

- There are three ways to build a business: (1) use a franchise model, (2) use trial and error, and (3) leverage a Management Blueprint. The latter cuts several years off the learning curve while giving a business owner maximum entrepreneurial flexibility for a modest investment.
- More than a hundred years of documented management theory and insights have yielded The Seven Management Concepts. These seven have stood the test of time. Leading management consultants and CEOs have implemented these concepts at most major corporations, and you can harvest this wisdom for your business.
- The Seven Management Concepts are (1) Culture, (2) Structure, (3) Vision, (4) Strategy, (5) Execution, (6) Process and (7) Alignment.
- Mastering these concepts and introducing them into your business represent gathering the low-hanging fruit that increase any organization's effectiveness.

USE A MANAGEMENT BLUEPRINT

Vision without execution is hallucination.

—THOMAS EDISON

In the summer of 2012, I was feeling mixed emotions. Notwithstanding my failure to sell MB Partners, my family was excited about the move to America. On June 19, we flew via London to Washington, D.C., with six pieces of luggage, two big ones for Dora and me, and a small one for each of our kids. At 45, I was ready to conquer the New World.

At Heathrow I picked up a copy of an intriguing book titled *Traction: Get a Grip on Your Business*, by Gino Wickman. It described the Entrepreneurial Operating System that would help me "get everything I wanted from my business."

I had devoured it by the time we landed at Dulles. Although I didn't call it a Management Blueprint then, I did realize that this book was like *The E-Myth*—a handbook on turning a business into a well-oiled machine.

My plan was to spend one week a month between Budapest and Bucharest visiting the two offices of MB Partners, helping to land new business, and to reassure my clients that our team would deliver what we promised. Although I was excited about what I had read in *Traction*, I didn't follow a formal implementation of EOS, but I did apply the tools as I saw fit.

On my first trip back, I sat down with my partners and we discussed how I would be away opening a US branch of MB Partners and that László, Róbert, and Levente would be in charge of general management, project execution, and sales, respectively. We would have a Skype meeting on Mondays to monitor key performance indicators and to make sure that the company was hitting its targets. I had the same conversation with Cosmin, who was running our Bucharest office.

I fretted about how the company would manage in my absence as I focused on building our branch office in Richmond, Virginia.

But my concerns were unfounded. My colleagues totally outperformed my expectations. They were executing like clockwork and signing up new clients, initially with my help and later in my absence. It was exhilarating, but I also felt redundant for apparently not being that important to MB Partners after all…

Things were going so well that 13 months after his original offer, Krisztián came back to the table with a much-improved proposal. In June 2013, the Oriens IM Group bought full control of MB Partners. At that moment, I realized that in *Traction* and EOS, Gino Wickman had created something special.

10 MANAGEMENT BLUEPRINTS

After our move and the sale of MB Partners, I built a CEO network in my new hometown and assembled two peer groups of business owners and CEOs of midsize companies. As a contractor of Vistage International, I facilitated monthly leadership meetings for these groups and coached the CEOs.

I would also invite speakers, curated by Vistage's speakers' bureau, to these meetings. Most presentations were informational and entertaining, and the speakers seemed to have a lot of fun presenting to these groups of entrepreneurs. I decided to follow in their footsteps and develop my own talks.

One topic that intrigued me was the idea of a "business blueprint": Which ones existed outside of *The E-Myth* and EOS? I found many others and, after much consideration, I narrowed down the field to 10 systems I consider holistic frameworks that businesses can apply to improve the management of their organizations.

In this chapter, I discuss these 10 Management Blueprints in chronological order of their original publication. You may implement any one of them using the book or online tools associated with it, or by hiring specialist consultants to professionally implement the program for you, walking you through the process.

Enacting a Management Blueprint at your company, where a cohesive management philosophy may be missing, will improve your business and move it toward buyability.

Enjoy the sightseeing.

THE PIONEERS

The E-Myth

The E-Myth: Why Most Small Businesses Don't Work and What to Do About It (1986) and *The E-Myth Revisited* (1995) by Michael Gerber

If your business depends on you, you don't own a business—you have a job. And it's the worst job in the world, as you are working for a lunatic.

—MICHAEL GERBER

The E-Myth was first published in 1986 as nonfiction and re-released in 1995 as business fable.

According to Michael Gerber, the e-myth, or entrepreneur myth, is that most companies are started by heroic business visionaries. However, in reality most businesses are launched by technicians, not entrepreneurs, and often by accident, rather than by design. This is why 50 percent of American businesses fail within five years.[36]

Gerber makes the case that to succeed, technicians must start working on their business as much as they work in it. Over time, they need to become managers and eventually entrepreneurs if they want to keep growing their business.

The other idea in *The E-Myth* is to follow the "McDonald's model," which entails systematizing your business into a replicable "franchise prototype" that you then can scale in other geographic locations, without you, the entrepreneur, having to be around to run these units.

The rest of the book draws an outline of the major steps for creating the franchise prototype, which includes strategies for accomplishing the following:

- Innovating, quantifying, and orchestrating the key processes of the business
- Determining your primary aim, what you want to achieve with your vision
- Painting a vision of your business, which Gerber calls the strategic objective
- Devising an organizational strategy around key functions, not personalities, and setting clear expectations with "position contracts"
- Creating a management system to find and keep customers by making expectations clear, creating processes, and "gamifying" them to keep employees engaged and focused
- Determining the demographics and psychographics of your target customers
- Designing a systems strategy that stipulates the visual appearance, processes, and management information required to build a functioning franchise prototype

In One Sentence

Upgrade technician-operated small service businesses to franchise effectiveness.

The Great Game of Business

The Great Game of Business: Unlocking the Power and Profitability of Open-Book Management (1992) and *A Stake in the Outcome* (2002), by Jack Stack

> *The best way to operate a business is to give everybody a voice in saying how the company is run and a stake in the financial outcome.*

> —JACK STACK

In 1983, 13 employees of International Harvester purchased a part of the company that rebuilt truck engines, called Springfield ReManufacturing Corporation (SRC).[37] They put in $100,000 in cash and assumed $8.9 million in loans; a share in SRC was worth 10 cents. Twenty-five years later, the SRC group's revenue had grown from $16 million to more than $1 billion, and the share price had multiplied more than 3,600 times.[38] SRC's founder and CEO, Jack Stack, memorialized their journey in two books: *The Great Game of Business* and *A Stake in the Outcome*. *The Great Game of Business* has sold 350,000 copies in 14 languages.[39]

Stack explains that the way SRC survived the early days and prospered thereafter was to gamify saving the company. He engaged and educated employees on how to interpret financial statements and metrics so that everyone could understand what was required and how they needed to contribute. They called it the Great Game of Business (GGOB) and later set up a subsidiary for teaching the method to other companies.

Stack believes that the game can work in any organization that has financial statements, because numbers are a way to tell a story about people and provide a way of keeping score. Traditional closed-book management companies ask people to play the game without being shown the score, which Stack considers absurd.[40]

The fundamental ideas of the GGOB blueprint include

- How to make money
- Telling the truth versus being a "nice guy"
- Starting games and celebrating wins

- Defining and sharing the big picture
- Addressing the fears of open-book management
- Focusing on critical numbers
- Designing an effective bonus program
- Involving employees in planning
- Making staff meetings effective
- The importance of equity ownership
- Healthcare cost and ownership

In One Sentence

Be honest and transparent with your people and teach them how to play the game and win together.

The Rockefeller Habits

Mastering the Rockefeller Habits: What You Must Do to Increase the Value of Your Growing Firm (2002) by Verne Harnish

If you want to teach people a new way of thinking, don't bother trying to teach them. Instead, give them a tool, which will lead to new ways of thinking.

— BUCKMINSTER FULLER

Verne Harnish studied as a mechanical engineer, after which he decided on a business career and earned an MBA. While studying at Wichita State University, he founded the Association of Collegiate Entrepreneurs and then expanded the concept nationally and later globally when, in 1987, he founded the Young Entrepreneurs Organization (now: EO).

Working and consulting with the members of EO in the following 15 years inspired Harnish to publish *Mastering the Rockefeller Habits*. His goal was to create a toolset of fundamental principles for running a great business.[41] He was inspired by John D. Rockefeller's leadership and management principles, GE's management philosophies, Jim Collins's Hedgehog Concept, and others.[42]

He picked up three habits from Rockefeller:

1. Set annual and quarterly priorities and a quarterly theme for the business.
2. Collect and use data to make sure the company is running effectively and delivers what the market demands.
3. Maintain organizational alignment using daily, weekly, quarterly, and annual meetings.

Harnish also embraces finding the choke point in the business and taking control of it. He mentions the example of Rockefeller's Standard Oil, which focused on gaining an advantage in railroad transportation costs, its own chokepoint.

Harnish uses the following ideas from General Electric:

- Ignore medium-term plans, have a long-term energizing goal, and focus on quarterly objectives.
- Keep everything stupidly simple. If your strategies, plans, decisions seem complicated, they are probably wrong.
- Get firsthand data. Keep close to your middle managers and your customers so you obtain real-time information directly from the source.

The Rockefeller Habits was the first Management Blueprint to introduce practical tools to readers, such as the Planning Pyramid, One Page Strategic Plan, Management Accountability Plan, and Weekly and Daily Meeting Structures. The approach is more structured than the Great Game of Business but still flexible enough to adopt as companies see fit.

In One Sentence
Grow your business using a handful of simple and proven principles and tools and regular, structured meetings.

THE CLASSICS

The Entrepreneurial Operating System
Traction: Get a Grip on Your Business (2007), by Gino Wickman

> *The real goal is 80 percent strong in the Six Key Components™,*
> *or better. If you're above that level, you have a well-oiled machine.*

— GINO WICKMAN

Gino Wickman joined his family sales training business at age 25. He soon discovered that his father was more of an entrepreneur than a manager, more excited about ideas, strategy, and clients than managing a profitable business. Gino jumped in and helped to right the ship and grow and sell the business.

Wickman seems to have embraced the tools of all the Management Blueprints that came before him, augmenting them along the way with concepts from Jim Collins, Dan Sullivan, Andy Grove, Patrick Lencioni, and others. His genius was to simplify many of these concepts and solidify them into a precise recipe that is easy to teach and follow.

Wickman created the EOS Model®, a graphical illustration of the Six Key Components of an entrepreneurial business: Vision, People, Data, issues, Process, and Traction, together with two tools and disciplines to strengthen each of these components. The EOS Model includes a measurement system to track progress toward achieving a great company that executes flawlessly.

He also simplified the deliverables of EOS to three words: Vision (full cultural and goal alignment), Traction (disciplined and accountable execution), and Healthy (creating functional and cohesive teams).

EOS uses the Pareto principle, simplifying the system to 20 tools and then designating five of them as "foundational" that, when adopted, advance companies 80 percent toward mastering the system.

He also came up with the concept of a proven process visual that enables users to see how they can implement EOS in their business. The goal is to ingrain EOS and make companies fully self-run within two years.

In One Sentence
Implement a proven process using practical tools and disciplines to create vision alignment, ingrain execution habits, and build a cohesive team.

Rapid Enterprise Development
The Breakthrough Company: How Everyday Companies Become Extraordinary Performers (2008), by Keith R. McFarland

> *It's not reckless to make ever-escalating bets on your company's future. The only safety comes in constantly upping the ante.*

—KEITH MCFARLAND

Keith McFarland, former CEO of an *Inc. 500* technology company, credits a chance meeting with Jim Collins for inspiring his research that led to *The Breakthrough Company*. McFarland replicated Collins's Good to Great process, conducted for the elite of the Fortune 500, and applied it to small, fast-growing companies. The Rapid Enterprise Development team gathered empirical research on nine companies and their competitors and interviewed more than 1,400 managers and executives from 52 client companies to learn the lessons McFarland shares in the book.[43]

Specifically, McFarland wanted to answer the question of why most small companies stay small while others traverse the entrepreneurial stage and grow large. Was there a way to increase the chances of that happening? The research yielded a handful of ideas:

- "Throw a dyno": A rock climber's term about making a willful and diligent ascent, from one foothold to the next.[44]
- "Crown the company": Let the story be about the business, not its founder.
- "Upping the ante": Keep making bold bets, because often the

winner takes all in the fast-growth world of tech companies.
- "Build company character": Implant and enforce a value-based culture.
- Navigate the "Bermuda Triangle": Balance innovation, customer service, and efficiency.
- "Erect scaffoldings": Embrace peer groups and "Insultants" that support and challenge you.
- Focus on the three leverage points: strategy, alignment, and execution: Engage more people in creating strategy, share information, and increase the velocity of feedback and learning.

In One Sentence

Implement a multifaceted and consultative strategic planning and organizational development program that engages multiple management layers in medium-size and large companies.

The Advantage

The Advantage: Why Organizational Health Trumps Everything Else in Business (2012), by Patrick Lencioni

> *If you could get all the people in an organization rowing in the same direction, you could dominate any industry, in any market, at any time.*
>
> —PATRICK LENCIONI

Patrick Lencioni is a management consultant and alumnus of Bain & Company and Oracle who struck out on his own and has published a dozen business books since 1998. He writes about team dynamics and how to make organizations perform better. Most of his books, such as *Five Dysfunctions of a Team*, are business fables.

The notable exception is *The Advantage*, which pulls together the key concepts from his fable books into a nonfiction Management Blueprint format.

Lencioni makes the case that although most CEOs are tweaking the dial to make their businesses "smarter," they are missing a much higher leverage opportunity, which is to make their organization "healthier." "The health of an organization provides context for strategy, finance, marketing and technology, which is why it is the single biggest factor determining an organization's success."[45]

According to Lencioni, three inherent biases against focusing on teamwork exist in the business world. The work is "not sophisticated" enough, it's warm and fuzzy stuff; it's not an adrenaline-inducing activity; and progress in team-health building is hard to measure. Business leaders often ask: What is the financial impact really of having a more cohesive leadership team? How can we justify to the board or even to ourselves spending time on it?

Miracle on Grass

Let me illustrate the importance of teamwork with a soccer analogy. In 2004, the Greek national squad qualified for the Euro, the premier European championship tournament of the best 16 national teams. Europe is home to the best soccer teams, and thus the Euro is the most competitive tournament in the world. Greece's qualification was a major surprise, and the Greek Soccer Association hired Otto Rehhagel, the winningest soccer coach in Germany, to avoid a disaster in the tournament.

Rehhagel surveyed the field of Greek soccer talent and decided on the only strategy that had any chance: building a defensive team. Scoring goals was a long shot, but perhaps they could avoid conceding too many of them and the Greek squad could keep their dignity.

One of the tournament's favorites, Portugal, hosted the Euro that year and, according to custom, opened the games by playing the lowest-ranking qualifier: Greece. We normally expect the hosts to win their opening game to get the local audience excited and kick off the tournament with a solid start.

This was not to be. Greece scored in the seventh minute of the opening game, and from a penalty, and won 2–1. The defeat humiliated the Portuguese team, but they rallied to win their subsequent matches and got through to the knockout stage. Greece tied another game and qualified behind them.

In the quarterfinals, Greece was up against the defender of the title, France. However, it was the heroically defending Greeks who scored from a header in the 65th minute.

Greece was through to the semifinals, where it met with the Czech Republic, the only team that had won all its games so far. Former Euro winners and runners-up, the Czechs were overwhelming favorites. But again, the Greeks triumphed with a golden goal header from a corner in extra time.

The final ended up being a rematch of Portugal and Greece. Star of the tournament and the most enduring star of all times, Cristiano Ronaldo led the charge, ready to recover Portuguese honor. But, again, it didn't happen. Greek teamwork once again overcame Portuguese brilliance, and with another corner header Greece became champion of the Euro.

If great teamwork can win the toughest soccer tournament in the world against the highest-paid star, don't you think it might help your business win more, too?

Now what has this got to do with Lencioni's Advantage? Even if teamwork is hard to quantify, excellent teams can perform miracles. Probably you have anecdotal evidence you trust from your own experiences.

Lencioni identifies four disciplines that create organizational health:

1. **Build a cohesive leadership team.** The fish rots from the head down, so the head is where you must start. A leadership team is collectively responsible for achieving a common aim.
2. **Create clarity.** Answer six critical questions: Why do you exist? How do you behave? What do you do? How will you succeed? What is most important right now? Who must do what?
3. **Overcommunicate clarity.** You must tell people seven times for them to believe in, internalize, and embrace your mission, values, and strategy.
4. **Reinforce clarity.** Institutionalize your culture without bureaucratizing it. Design human systems to tie operations, culture, and management together.

In One Sentence

Improve your organization by building a cohesive leadership team, clarifying and overcommunicating your vision, and coding it into your people processes.

Scaling Up

Scaling Up: How a Few Companies Make It...and Why the Rest Don't (2014), by Verne Harnish

> *Everything should be made as simple as possible, but no simpler.*
>
> —ALBERT EINSTEIN

Following the publication of *Traction*, Verne Harnish came up with "Rockefeller Habits 2.0" and titled it *Scaling Up*. This is a system directed at strengthening fast-growth companies that is organized around four areas: people, strategy, execution, and cash.

In *Scaling Up*, Harnish updated the One Page Strategic Plan and added a thinking tool he calls the 7 Strata of Strategy, which includes "the word you own in the mind of your customer," "brand promises," a "guarantee," your "one-phrase strategy" that upsets your competitors, your "differentiating activities," and establishing and measuring your "Profit per X" economic driver, which he borrowed from Jim Collins.

The updated Rockefeller system also includes six new tools, such as the One-Page Personal Plan, the Process Accountability Chart, and a modified strengths, weaknesses, opportunities, and threats (SWOT) analysis called SWT, to identify strengths, weaknesses, and trends. Also included is a 40-point Rockefeller Habits Checklist to ensure your business is functioning at peak levels.

The brand-new section "Cash" includes seven financial levers to pull to increase cash flow and profitability and a Cash Acceleration Strategies worksheet.

Harnish makes a passing reference to other authors who have copied and, in the process, "over-simplified" parts of the Rockefeller Habits system, which causes them to leave money on the table. Therefore, *Scaling Up* may have been an attempt to add the valuable meat back onto the bone.

In One Sentence

A complete strategy and execution toolkit for medium-size companies aspiring for fast, cash-efficient growth.

THE THIRD WAVE

4DX

The 4 Disciplines of Execution: Achieving Your Wildly Important Goals (2016) by Chris McChesney, Sean Covey, and Jim Hulling

The 4 Disciplines of Execution (4DX) program, created by FranklinCovey, drives organizational results through behavior change. The 4DX program focuses on articulating your major, definite objective, the one it calls the Wildly Important Goal (WIG or The War) and then breaking it down into a handful of "WIG Battles" and quarterly execution steps. The process includes keeping a weekly scoreboard of lead measures for each team participant and monitoring performance using a cadence of weekly, monthly, and quarterly meetings.

Simply put, if your Big Hairy Audacious Goal (BHAG) is the *what* of your organization, the process of execution is the *how*. The authors argue that most leaders find strategy much easier than execution; strategy is what major MBA programs focus on as well. This is not surprising because strategy "only" takes analysis, frameworks, and smart people putting their heads together, whereas execution requires lasting behavioral change.

The book quotes W. Edwards Deming, the father of the quality movement, as saying, "When the majority of the people behave in a certain way, the problem is systemic." Execution is the key to your people understanding the organization's strategy in the first place.

The authors commissioned Harris Interactive to survey employees at hundreds of businesses and governmental agencies and found that the major reason for a failure of execution was lack of goal clarity:

1. 85 percent of the people surveyed did not understand the goal of their organization,
2. 49 percent were not committed to that goal when it was stated,
3. 81 percent were not held accountable to reaching their organization's goal, and
4. 87 percent had no idea how they personally contributed to achieving that goal.

In other words, most of the people surveyed were caught up in the whirlwind of daily emergencies and had no bandwidth left to dedicate to progressing their organizations.

In One Sentence

Drive your organization forward by prioritizing one or two simple, big goals; measure their execution through personalized lead measures; and hold people accountable using regular meetings.

OKRs

Measure What Matters: How Google, Bono, and the Gates Foundation Rock the World with OKRs (2018), by John Doerr

An effective goal-setting system starts with disciplined thinking at the top, with leaders who invest the time and energy to choose what counts.

—JOHN DOERR

John Doerr is an electrical engineer who started at Andy Grove's Intel, which he left to become one of the most successful venture capitalists in America. He has backed Amazon, AOL, Compaq, Google, Netscape, Twitter, and Slack.[46] Doerr took Andy Grove's objectives and key results (OKRs) management tool with him and introduced it to Sun Microsystems in 1980 and a startup called Google in 1999.[47] From there, it grew into a standard management staple of Silicon Valley.

OKRs are a collaborative goal-setting protocol for companies, teams, and individuals. The first part of OKRs, objectives, represent what you want to do (launch a killer game!); key results (KRs) are how you know whether you've achieved them (downloads of 25K/day, revenue of $50K/day).

Effective key results are specific, time-bound, aggressive yet realistic, measurable, and verifiable. Whereas objectives can be long-lived, lasting for a year or longer, key results change as the work progresses.[48] An effective goal management system links goals to a team's broader mission. It moves people to strive for what might seem beyond reach.

For larger companies, OKRs become the themes of the quarter, set by the top management team and cascaded to the organization. Company OKRs allow teams and individuals lower down in the organization to establish their own OKRs that contribute to the quarterly themes.

Google makes all OKRs transparent to everyone in the organization, creating accountability and clarity. Everyone is privy to what everyone else is working on and understands their contributions and any interdependencies.

Fast-growing tech companies like Google, LinkedIn, and Zynga set both "committed OKRs," expecting 100 percent completion, and "aspirational OKRs," which they grade "green" and celebrate when more than 70 percent complete. For slower-growth businesses, setting committed OKRs is the norm. (The version of OKRs used in Scaling Up and EOS, called "Rocks," is the equivalent of committed OKRs.)

Doerr enumerates the mistakes in writing OKRs and encourages business leaders to avoid the following traps:

1. Confusing OKRs cause failure or priority inversion.
2. Sandbagging is when committed OKRs are not fully consumed or aspirational OKRs are stretched.
3. Setting low-value, "who cares" objectives doesn't move the needle.
4. When key results are insufficient for committed objectives, a fully completed OKR will fail to deliver.

Doerr introduces the concept of CFRs to help test OKRs. CFR stands for conversations (between manager and contributor driving results), feed-back (bidirectional or with peers to evaluate progress), and recognition (appreciation of deserving contributions of individuals). CFRs are especially important for evaluating the partial accomplishments of moon-shot-sized aspirational key results.

In One Sentence

Drive organizational priorities and communicate in your fast-growing business by setting, cascading, and evaluating objectives and key results.

The 3HAG Way

The Metronome Effect (2014) and *The 3HAG Way* (2018) by Shannon Byrne Susko

Like Gino Wickman, Shannon Byrne Susko started as a member of Verne Harnish's Gazelle program and she was inculcated in Rockefeller Habits and Scaling Up principles. Her system, documented in her two books, evolved from Scaling Up's toolset. However, there are some notable differences.

Susko recognizes the significance of articulating the business leader's personal vision before creating a Jim Collins-esque BHAG for the company.

She also tweaks Harnish's 3-5 Year Plan into a "3HAG" (3-Year Highly Achievable Goal), which she modifies into a 36-month rolling plan. This plan is designed to develop your company toward achieving its five strategic differentiators that make it uniquely valuable and better than key competitors.

She suggests designing your 3HAG Plan using a handful of strategic tools. She developed these at two tech companies she ran, and they are based on concepts derived from Jim Collins, Michael E. Porter, and other management and strategy thinkers.

Her most interesting strategy tools are the following:

1. **Attribution Framework**: A matrix that contrasts your company

against its competitors based on product features critical to your ideal customer.

2. **Activity Fit Map**: A tool to determine Five Strategic Differentiators you want to develop in order to stand out in the field, to be then synthesized into your **One Phrase Strategy.**

3. **Market Map**: This tool helps you map out your go-to-market and supply chain strategies and your differentiated niche. It is based on Porter's Five Forces model and shows how your business depends on and interacts with its competitors, suppliers, partners, distribution channels, and customers.

4. **Swimlanes**: A 12-calendar quarter milestone plan you can use to upgrade the features of each of your Five Strategic Differentiators (mapped above) that will help you to win against your competitors.

5. **Key Process Flow Map**: This plots how each function in your business makes money and accelerates your cash flow.

In One Sentence

A tuned-up version of Scaling Up with heavy use of strategy tools and a rolling three-year planning process.

KEY IDEAS

- You can leverage a Management Blueprint as a shortcut to creating a self-managing, growing, profitable, and scalable business.
- The 10 Management Blueprints include **the pioneers**: the E-Myth and the Great Game of Business; **the classics**: Rockefeller Habits, EOS, Rapid Enterprise Development, and The Advantage; and **the third wave**: 4DX, OKRs and the 3HAG Way.
- Each blueprint has its own target audience, emphasizes specific aspects of entrepreneurship and management, and offers various tools you can use to implement some or all of The Seven Management Concepts.

6

HOW MANAGEMENT BLUEPRINTS WORK

Clarify your vision and you will make better decisions about people, processes, finances, strategies, and customers.

—GINO WICKMAN

In early October 2017, my long-term coaching and EOS client Jeremy Ford called me.

"We won it!" Jeremy exclaimed.

Won what? I wondered.

"We just topped the RVA 25 ranking for being the fastest-growing business in Central Virginia!" he said.

Two years earlier, Jeremy had taken over a failing fire and water damage remediation business that he had renamed RVA Restoration, as a way to identify with the city of Richmond in Virginia where it operated. The then co-owner, construction entrepreneur Shane Burnette, had hired me to coach him. Inspired by Shane, Jeremy had switched from a corporate career with Travelers Insurance. The business took off like a rocket and after two short years Jeremy bought out his shareholders. And later in that year, his company won the RVA 25, Richmond's yearly ranking of the region's fastest-growing companies, and stayed on the list for two more years as its revenue surpassed $6 million, with 45 employees.

How could a first-time entrepreneur with an all-newbie leadership team create a fast-growing company in a traditional blue-collar business in record time? RVA Restoration's leading peers took 10 to 15 years to grow to that size.

RVA Restoration's is a talented and passionate team that leveraged a Management Blueprint. They chose EOS.

After a rusty and confused start, when they were off track with all their Scorecard measurables, they were hitting 12 of 13 in the last quarter. Jeremy's team now has a clear vision and full alignment across the company. While competitors are struggling to find capable hires, RVA Restoration has a wait list of word-of-mouth applicants. Their people are the right people in the right seats, and the team addresses any people issues by coaching people up or out of the company.

All RVA employees identify issues and prioritize and solve them every week. Only the thorniest of these filter up to the leadership team; the rest are nipped in the bud by lower-level associates.

The company has also documented its core processes and has a system in place to make sure that the processes are being followed and regularly refined.

And the top team gets together every quarter to review what they have achieved, identify meaty issues and opportunities, set priorities, and solve problems. After the meeting, they gather everyone together and tell them what they have done, what they have decided, and the themes of the coming quarter. RVA Restoration keeps gaining traction every quarter.

As we discussed earlier, Peter Drucker, Jim Collins, Andy Grove, and others have articulated Seven Management Concepts that help you build a self-managing, growing, and profitable business. In the last chapter, we reviewed 10 Management Blueprints that package these concepts into digestible form for the consumption of entrepreneurs who run small and medium-size private companies.

In this chapter, we will review how various Management Blueprints turn these concepts into practical tools that can be implemented without hiring a Harvard MBA, retaining McKinsey and Company for a king's ransom, or bringing in a private equity fund manager to figure things out.

THE FOUNDATION

You can't build a great building on a weak foundation.
You must have a solid foundation if you are going to have
a strong superstructure.

—GORDON B. HINCKLEY

Concept 1: Culture

There are two critical elements to building a great culture for your business. First, it requires you to define the ***core values*** that drive the behavior of your people and hold yourself and others accountable to living them. Second, you have to build a ***healthy organization*** where people are willing to be vulnerable and honest with each other, and commit to and be accountable to the goals of your company.

Core Values

Since the publication of Jim Collins and William Lazier's *Beyond Entrepreneurship* in 1992, consensus has formed around the concept of core values. These values, in many cases implanted by a company's founding entrepreneur, are the inherent guiding principles that govern the behaviors of the people who drive the organization forward.

From the beginning, founders naturally surround themselves with people who share their values. However, as a business grows and the entrepreneurs are gradually distanced from hiring, their values do not automatically remain part of the selection process. This is where articulating, defining, and institutionalizing core values come into play.

Core vs. Corporate Values. As setting core values became fashionable and coining politically correct values became a staple service of management consultants around the turn of the millennium, the concept gradually became depersonalized. Companies started picking aspirational company values that reflected corporate expediency, rather than the historic virtues of these organizations. According to an *Inc.* magazine article[49], the recent most popular core values of the *Fortune* 500 have been: integrity (55 percent of companies state this is one of their core values), teamwork, innovation, customer service, and respect.

Unfortunately, these are *corporate* rather than *core* values. They are abstract concepts that don't inform the expected behaviors of the people inside the organization; also, these days they have little more than questionable PR value.

Discovering Your Core Values. Your business's core values are the organization's guiding principles that have helped your company come this far. Founders share their core values with their best people, possibly even inculcate people with these values—the business's best people live and breathe the core values.

Whatever your core values are, they represent your business's identity. By discovering and amplifying these values, you can attract the right kind of people to your organization. Over time, your business will exude these values and your customers will feel them, without having to be told what they are.

In *The Advantage*, Patrick Lencioni warns of three traps to dodge when setting values.[50] First, avoid picking aspirational values, that is, standards that are not already inherent in your company. Proclaiming such as-yet-unachieved values as core is hypocritical. The second trap is selecting values that represent a minimum standard in your industry, such as "integrity"—although for some companies like Enron, such a value turned out to be aspirational. The third mistake to avoid is emphasizing an accidental value that may have been prevalent but that is no longer relevant to the company's future, such as what often happens with "entrepreneurialism" in institutionalizing a business.[51]

Picking Aspirational Values Will Backfire. Two years ago I helped a large professional association implement the Entrepreneurial Operating System. When it came time to pick core values, the organization selected

"Does the Right Thing" on the insistence of its freshly minted CEO. When we tried to confirm whether the leadership team exhibited that value, several leaders refused to play along. The head of HR even insinuated that she was aware of ethical breaches that could not be shared with the group. The CEO decided to table the discussion and seal up that can of worms.

Verne Harnish, in *Mastering the Rockefeller Habits*, suggests using Jim Collins's Mission to Mars exercise to articulate your core values.[52] Ask your executive team to name three to five people who manifest the best traits and behaviors of the company and who they would send to Mars as emissaries of your company. After selecting the Mars team, the executives describe the positive behaviors and qualities of these people, and from that list the team synthesizes three to six behaviors as well as guiding principles that describe the DNA of your business.

Real core values allow you to see what it is like to be successful for your company and allow you to hold your people accountable to living up to these standards. Some of the flesh-and-blood values my clients have picked include: Hungry for Success, Willing to Help and Teach Others, Gets Shit Done, Engages with Content, Curious and Innovative, Willing to Adapt and Evolve, Impact Driven, and Critical Thinker.

These core values then become the basis for recruitment, selection, and appraisals. It is your job as the leader to make your core values come alive through examples and storytelling on a regular basis. You have to over-communicate your core values to make them stick over time.

Building a Healthy Organization

As you grow your business, you must work on building trust at all levels. You need people on your leadership team to openly address issues and challenges instead of politicking in the corridors of your organization.

At least once a year I talk each of my clients through Lencioni's Five Dysfunctions Pyramid,[53] which demonstrates that organizational health depends on building vulnerability-based trust between individuals. Only trusting teams are willing to confront each other to explore sensitive issues, commit to and be accountable for executing nonconsensus decisions, and take personal responsibility for the overall results of your company. If trust is weak, none of the above happens and leaders instead retreat to silos to defend their status and ego and to build their personal empires.

When you have clarified core values and laid the foundation for a healthy organization, it is time to figure out the right structure for your company.

Concept 2: Structure

It is almost always worth rethinking the organizational structure of your business. Most entrepreneurial companies evolve organically around the skills of early employees and seek to replace vacant functions with similarly skilled successors—but that can be a mistake because your business may not require the same function anymore and a different skillset might be more appropriate.

Figure Out What Your Business Needs

After starting MB Partners, it took me eight months to attract the first executive employee to my business, and I was lucky to find him. His name was Levente, and *he* actually found *me*. We met through a professional association I was running at the time, when he referred a friend of his family to me as a potential client. After they signed up, I asked Levente to help me serve them, and a few months later he became my first employee and eventually business partner. Levente was a great partner, but I did not define his job in advance and did not pick him to fit a specific job. Instead, I built a job around him.

Since Levente did a good job, I subsequently looked for more people like him, instead of defining the functions we needed, and we ended up with a lopsided team. This meant that I could only delegate transactional work and kept doing marketing, administration, finance, technology, and HR myself. Instead, I should have let go of lower value functions to others early, and spent my time on high-value activities, such as developing new business, cultivating key relationships, and building the company.

As the business owner, you can't afford to spend time on $50 per hour work. Start with a clean slate and consider the most important functions your business needs and the results you want from these functions. You will find that there are people you can hire or retain to execute these functions at a fraction of the cost of your time. There are people out there who are passionate about and expert on these functions and will execute them faster and better than you ever could.

Don't Confuse Owners and Managers

Michael Gerber in *The E-Myth* suggests separating owners from employees, to protect the organization from any confusion that may be caused by disagreements at the ownership level. Gerber calls the person who runs the business the Chief Operating Officer (COO). This individual reports to the shareholders and should be empowered to run the business on their behalf. She should manage the major functions that include marketing, operations, and finance and brake ties when there is no consensus. Sometimes, instead of the shareholders, the COO reports to a CEO who is the entrepreneur in the business and is the person who drives strategy and maintains key relationships.

Gino Wickman and Mark C. Winters in *Rocket Fuel* call the big-picture entrepreneurial leader at the top of the company the Visionary™ and their second in command, who runs the business, the Integrator.™

Figure 6.1 Gerber's Organization Chart

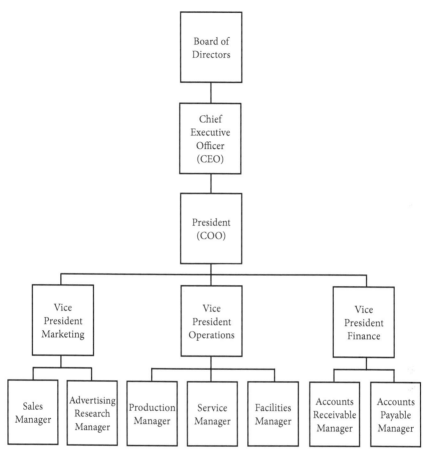

Source: Michael Gerber, *The E-Myth: Why Most Small Businesses Don't Work and What to Do About It* (New York: Harper & Row, 1986), 101.

Clarify Who Is Accountable for What

Verne Harnish in *Scaling Up* describes the function accountability chart, where each major function and a single owner for that function are defined. Each owner becomes accountable for the results of their function, including a key metric that measures its most important deliverable.

Similarly, Gerber recommends writing "position contracts" to define the results you expect from each major function on the organizational chart. A position contract provides each person with a sense of commitment and accountability because it communicates that the company is counting on each position owner to deliver.

Harnish goes one step further and suggests mapping each function's metric to respective lines on the profit and loss statement or balance sheet. That is accountability on steroids, and most companies will not need to go so far. At least not in the beginning.

Gino Wickman in EOS straddles the far ends and takes a middle course between Gerber and Harnish. EOS teaches you to define the major functions and their corresponding roles and then to put a person in the seat who understands the function, desires to own it, and has learned the abilities to execute it.

Don't Remove Yourself Too Early

Most entrepreneurs I meet aspire to be a visionary owner, one who needs not dirty their hands managing the day-to-day. Many think appointing an executive to manage the business (an Integrator) will make this happen. But this strategy can fizzle if you remove yourself from a growing business too soon.

For example, the owner of a construction company in Virginia Beach, I will call James, fell into this trap. In the first EOS meeting I facilitated for his company, he promoted his operation head, Ted, to the position of Integrator. Unfortunately, the gambit backfired when Ted was unable to delegate his duties in the Operations function to free himself for the Integrator job.

James also could not hold himself to the new reporting line and reached out to Ted's subordinates, who then naturally prioritized his requests over Ted's agenda, undercutting Ted in the process. When Ted thus became powerless to run the business, James was forced to demote him and take over running the business at the cost of great frustration to him, loss of face for Ted, and confusion to his operational leadership team. If your internal candidates are not yet ready to delegate, you are often better off hiring an experienced Integrator even if they will face a learning curve coming into the company.

Designing an organizational structure will help your business empower function owners to grow their areas like "mini CEOs." You may find that you cannot yet afford to shed too many hats. However, this exercise will help you identify your highest-leverage hires and prioritize them.

Empower the Right People

Elevating the owner to Visionary, even apparently prematurely, often pays off, however. Ethan Giffin, the owner of Groove Commerce, realized that he hit capacity and created a leadership team on the first day of Groove's EOS implementation. Ethan had a young, relatively inexperienced team of smart and high-EQ individuals who were eager to step up into more autonomous roles. They were ready to leave their respective comfort zones, and Ethan was no longer alone with solving the challenges of growing his e-commerce business.

Within 12 months, Groove turned the corner and made a profit after struggling to stay in the black during the previous four years. When his expanded leadership team started making faster and better decisions, staff turnover fell through the floor and morale skyrocketed.

Watch for Emerging Bottlenecks

Likewise, growing companies often outgrow their initial organizational arrangement when leaders reach their capacity barriers. Mike Michalowicz in *Clockwork* talks about the ideal mix of "designing, delegating, deciding, and doing." When an individual leader gets stuck making too many decisions and coaching too many direct reports, their widening span of control can upset any balance in that ideal mix. Pay attention to emerging bottlenecks by rethinking the business's organization regularly, anticipating needs to delegate, and consequently promote and hire people.

Wearing too many hats won't just slow growth but also make the "hat collector" indispensable—and the business consequently unbuyable. When building MB Partners, I held on to the management, finance, sales, marketing, and delivery functions much too long. When it came to selling my business, my "buyer" rightfully concluded that if I were to leave, there was going to be no business left to buy. I had to lose all my functional hats first, to make the business Buyable in the eyes of my potential investors.

The best thing to do is to design your ideal business structure 6 to 12 months ahead and focus on transitioning to the new setup by the time you need it. This requires some preparation, and you'll have to invest time into training incoming leaders, but the often-invisible payoff is undisrupted growth.

THE DIRECTION

*It is the set of the sails, not the direction of the wind
that determines which way we will go.*

—JIM ROHN

Concept 3: Vision

Whatever your mind can conceive and believe, it can achieve

—NAPOLEON HILL

Visioning is at center page in 7 of the 10 Management Blueprints discussed in Chapter 5. Without a vision, it is hard to see how a company can grow fast and achieve great things. At best, a visionless business grows in a reactive fashion driven by the fear of failure. At worst, it is consumed by complacency, and then drifts and loses momentum.

The Three Legs of Your Vision Stool

Your vision should consist of three elements. First, your aspirational purpose or mission, which is the equivalent of the Ideal Life for your business. What is the ultimate ideal your business is aspiring to achieve? Tesla's mission is to "To accelerate the world's transition to sustainable energy."

The second element is what Jim Collins calls the Big Hairy Audacious Goal, or BHAG. This should be your long-term milestone, 7 to 25 years out, en route to achieving your mission or purpose. For Tesla it is: "To produce 20 million electric vehicles a year before 2030."

The third piece of your vision is what Cameron Herold calls Vivid Vision. A medium-term detailed picture of your organization painted in Technicolor. This mental image is seared into the minds of your people and points to what must be manifested in the next few years. As of 2020, for Tesla, it is a 56 percent reduction in costs for batteries with a 50 percent longer range in addition to developing a US$25,000 Tesla model for the masses. (A Model T for the 21st century.)

Your Business's Purpose or Mission

It's a common misconception that a business exists to make money for its stakeholders, although many shareholders actually believe this. Passive stockholders are likely not interested in what the business is about as long as the stock performs and pays a dividend. Many employees see businesses simply as their paycheck. Ultimately, though, no business could make money without delivering value to society for which it can be paid—be it providing a funeral service, manufacturing widgets, distributing goods, or providing utilities.

Most businesses neglect to capitalize on the real benefit they provide to society, and thereby lose a huge opportunity to harness the mental and emotional energy of their employees. People are generally starved for meaning in their lives, and being able to contribute to a worthwhile cause can be immensely valuable to them. This is why dedicated teachers and nurses are willing to work at comparatively low wages while oil rig workers and morticians are paid much more for emotionally unrewarding jobs. It's worth digging deep to discover a worthwhile purpose for your business because it can potentially light up your workforce.

From Dirty Laundry to Green Champ. One of my former clients, Edward, who operated a laundry business cleaning hospital and hotel linen, vented his frustration about his hiring challenges. He attributed his inability to find good people on his business being an unrewarding one. Moving dirty linen in and out of industrial laundromats was uninspiring work, he said, and made it nigh impossible for him to attract millennial talent.

When Edward and his CEO peer group drilled down to find the "why" of the laundry business, they stumbled on a breakthrough. It turned out that by providing fresh, clean linen to hotel guests and hospital patients, Edward's business was providing the comfort of cleanliness and sanitation. Further, it was discovered that Edward's company used advanced environmentally friendly cleaning agents, while most of his competitors laundered using toxic chemicals. From there, it was easy to articulate a highly attractive purpose for the company. Edward soon attracted two talented executives who helped him reinvigorate and rejuvenate the management of his drifting family business.

A great vision exerts a gravitational pull on people. The tension between the present reality and the future purpose and vision is designed to create a sense of urgency and a level of excitement in your people, who are now tasked with a worthwhile undertaking. John F. Kennedy's grand vision, which he announced to a joint session of Congress in 1961, was that "this nation should commit itself to achieving the goal, before this decade is out, of landing a man on the moon and returning him safely to the earth." This vision mobilized and unified the country to achieve a dramatic accomplishment that has not been equaled in 50 years.

Your BHAG

The right kind of vision inspires employees of an organization to take action. Jim Collins and Jerry Porras in *Built to Last* argue that BHAGs must be aligned with an organization's purpose and represent a milestone along the way to achieving this purpose.

As an example, Elon Musk founded SpaceX in 2002 with the purpose of "reducing space transportation costs to enable the colonization of Mars." In 2017, Musk announced a BHAG as a waypoint en route to fulfilling SpaceX's purpose: His company would start earth-to-earth test flights by 2022, which would allow a SpaceX Starship craft to transport passengers from London to Hong Kong in 34 minutes. Rockets for earth-to-earth travel would be launched and landed at terminals easily accessible from major cities via high-speed boats or high-speed trains called Hyperloops.

As the acronym indicates, a BHAG must be audacious, such as SpaceX's earth-to-earth travel, to capture the imagination of your people. Incremental goals that can be achieved at the current level of thinking and technology won't inspire. An audacious goal represents a worthy challenge that will force dramatic innovation and even inventions to accomplish.

BHAGs must also be clearly articulated so that people can visualize them in their mind's eye. Ambiguous BHAGs that leave people wondering whether they were really achieved are unhelpful. For example, "revolutionizing space travel" would not be a clear BHAG for SpaceX because it is too vague to picture and too intangible to pursue.

Your Vivid Vision

Your BHAG is huge and you don't yet know how to achieve it, so you need something nearer term to sink your teeth into. This is your Vivid Vision, approximately three years out. It is a mental picture of your business that helps you make commensurate progress toward your Big Hairy Audacious Goal.

Herold recommends that you draft a two- to three-page narrative of what your business is going to look like three years from now. What will your revenues and profit be and how many employees will you have? What products and services will you offer in what geographies? What will the structure of your organization look like? Which technologies will you be leveraging? What kind of strategic partnerships will you have? What will your thought leadership look like and how will you relate to your community of customers? Answers to these types of questions form your Vivid Vision.

The Vivid Vision forms the link between your vision and strategic plan. It manifests your strategy of moving toward your BHAG and drives your priorities for the next few years.

With your purpose, BHAG, and Vivid Vision in hand, it's time to make your vision real with planning your strategy.

Concept 4: Strategy

Strategic planning is how you formulate the plan of action and policies to achieve the Vivid Vision you've painted for your business. It is also how you allocate the needed financial and people resources and plan for how these actions and policies would be implemented.

The five stages of the strategic planning process are as follows:

1. Analyze the internal and external environments of your business.
2. Formulate strategies to achieve your vision using conceptual frameworks.
3. Set goals.
4. Procure the financial and material resources and the right people to execute your goals.
5. Monitor, measure, and ensure that your strategic plan is implemented.

Analyze Your Environment with the ABCDEF Toolkit

The goal of this stage is to survey the field and enumerate all internal and external factors that can or should influence your strategy. Consider using the following tools:

A. Review the strengths, weaknesses, opportunities, and threats facing your business (**SWOT analysis**).
B. Evaluate the external environment for political, economic, social, technological, legal, and environmental impacts (**PESTLE analysis**).
C. Consider potential threats from suppliers, customers, competitors, substitutes, and new entrants (**Porter's Five Forces evaluation**).
D. Assess opportunities to improve your processes and your supply chain, from acquiring raw materials through final purchases by end users (**Value Chain analysis**; see Figure 6.2).
E. Assess how gaining experience could reduce production cost and improve competitiveness as you scale production and customer adoption (**Experience Curve assessment**).
F. Conduct industry and **market research**, customer surveys, **and competitive intelligence**.

Figure 6.2 Value Chain Analysis

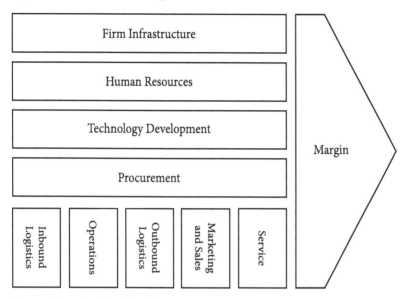

Source: Amanda Athuraliya, https://creately.com/blog/diagrams/what-is-a-strategy-map/.

Pull Eight Levers to Formulate Your Strategy

After synthesizing the information you have collected, it's time to pull out your strategic toolkit. Thankfully, the Management Blueprints discussed in Chapter 5 have produced over two dozen strategic thinking tools that you can leverage to devise your strategy.

Your most important strategic levers include answers to the following questions:

1. What is **your core competency**, which Jim Collins refers to as "what you can become the best at in the world"?
2. Who are **your ideal customers**, the people who will most benefit from your offering at a healthy profit margin?
3. What are **your strategic differentiators**, the characteristics that make you better than your peers in the eyes of these ideal customers?

4. What is **your geographic footprint**? Are you a local business, national, regional, or global?

5. What is **your market niche**, the niche where you are most competitive but with enough room for your growth plans?

6. What are **your two of three focus areas** out of operational excellence, innovation, and customer intimacy? (Hint: You can't be great at all three.)

7. Which of your offerings are **cash cows, stars, question marks, or dogs** and what will you do about them?

8. What are the **possible scenarios facing your business** and how will you navigate each if it came to pass?

No strategic planning can dispense with sound strategic thinking. These tools will help you reveal the dots, but you will have to do the thinking yourself to connect the dots into a coherent strategy that will lead you to manifesting your Vivid Vision.

Set Annual Goals

Having formulated a clear strategy, it's time to set goals for the coming year. What themes will help you make the required progress toward your three-year Vivid Vision?

Great goal setting requires naming a limited number of meaningful objectives that will challenge your team. A good rule of thumb is to calibrate your goals to a 90 percent effort to accomplish. That way, you leave room to handle inevitable contingencies without burning out your people. But if you set the bar lower, your goals won't energize your team and you risk procrastination and the loss of momentum.

More than three to five goals will either overwhelm your team or the goals will end up too small to make a difference. The best goals are broad, take the business to a new level, and require concerted effort to accomplish by multiple areas of your company throughout the year.

One of my clients, a fast-growing technology firm, set the following three goals for the year:

1. Build, train, and launch a Customer Success team.
2. Create a data analytics business line with a new product that existing customers want.
3. Develop a cloud offering piloted with 10 paying customers.

They set "only" three goals, but each one is strategic, game-changing, and challenging enough to make the teamwork hard the whole year. The team will also have plenty to celebrate when they have completed these goals.

Resource the Plan

When you establish challenging goals that require people to stretch and grow, you need to provide the extra resources needed. Who do you need to hire and what financing do you need to obtain to support the expansion?

It is critical that you hire the right people who fit your culture and can get the job done. Consider using personality assessment tools, such as Kolbe, DISC, or Predictive Index. Topgrading by Bradford Smart is another excellent methodology to draw on. Some of these tools cost money, but they will save you time and stress by turning a hit-and-miss recruiting process into a mostly scientific one.

A good strategic plan that makes sense to investors will help fund your growth. Keep your eyes and ears open to the approaches that your board and venture investors use to evaluate your strategy and come up with a plan they can relate to.

Control the Implementation

Several Management Blueprint tools can help you steer the implementation of your strategic plan.

One is the Strategy Map, created by Robert S. Kaplan and David P. Norton as part of their Balanced Scorecard framework. (See Figure 6.2). It helps develop and display your strategy at the leadership level. It also helps the leadership team articulate a coherent story in order to explain your strategy to employees, and it helps everyone in the business understand how they contribute to moving the organization forward.

113

Figure 6.3 Strategy Map

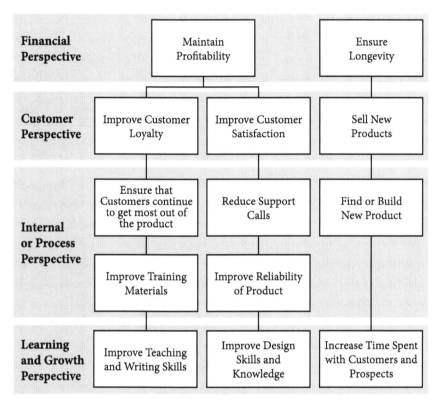

Source: "What Is a Strategy Map?" Visual Paradigm Online, https://online.visual-paradigm.com/knowledge/strategic-map/what-is-strategy-map/.

Now that your strategy is clear, it is time to execute it.

THE PRODUCTION

Don't mistake activity with achievement.

—JOHN WOODEN

Concept 5: Execution

Business execution means engaging the employees of an organization in carrying out the necessary tasks in an organized and disciplined fashion to accomplish your strategic plan.

The Management Blueprint laser-focused on that subject is the *4 Disciplines of Execution* (4DX) introduced in Chapter 5. The authors of 4DX argue that you should master the following four disciplines to become great at business execution:

1. Focus on the "wildly important."
2. Act on lead measures.
3. Keep a compelling scoreboard.
4. Create a cadence of accountability.

Focus on the "Wildly Important"

Do less to achieve more. Ambitious, smart leaders want to accomplish more than possible and therefore they often fragment their efforts. The sun's scattered rays are too weak to start a fire, but focused with a magnifying glass, they will light up a flame in seconds. You need a forcing function in your business to reduce the number of "priorities" and to make sure they are accomplished in their order of importance.

With your annual plan complete, it is time to break it down and plan your first quarter. What will be your revenue, profit, and key strategic metric in the next three months, and what are your business's three to five priorities for the next quarter that move you along toward your one-year goals? Prioritize the most powerful initiatives to get meaningful results for

115

your business. You must make sure that these are SMART priorities, that is, they are specific, measurable, attainable, realistic, and time-bound. John Doerr calls these priorities OKRs (see Chapter 5), and Scaling Up and Traction call them Rocks.

Verne Harnish, author of *Mastering the Rockefeller Habits*, was the first to call these priorities Rocks, a term he picked up from Stephen Covey, who wrote the iconic *7 Habits of Highly Effective People*. Covey taught business school classes at Utah State University, and he would demonstrate in class using two glass cylinders and piles of rocks, pebbles, and sand what prioritization meant.

Rock, Pebbles, and Sand. Pebbles represent the urgent and important tasks that you have to tackle every day: serving clients, meeting deadlines, putting out fires. Rocks symbolize the big, important initiatives that move a company forward; they may not always seem as urgent as pebbles. And then you have the sand, which stands for all the interruptions and distractions, such as making cold calls and writing emails, checking sports scores, posting on social media, and chatting around the water cooler, which feel important but are not.

Entropy pushes most people to start with the sand, which are attractive tasks, and then turn to the pebbles, the urgent things staring them in the face. By 4 p.m., when they have put out the fires, the cylinder is almost full of sand and pebbles—there is no room for rocks. The "entropy people" feel burned out and lack the mental energy to tackle the big, non-routine projects, which are the truly important ones.

Contrast this with the focused approach. Put the rocks in the cylinder—the initiatives that are crucial to moving your business forward—first thing each morning for an hour or two, when you are still fresh to solve problems and make decisions. Then get down to tackling your pebbles to keep clients and bosses happy. All your pebbles are in the cylinder by 4 p.m., when you still have time left for socializing and relaxing (sand) before heading home. The pebbles fall through the gaps in the rocks, and the sand sifts in to fill the remaining voids. Everything fits.

Set Quarterly Priorities. After your annual plan is complete, and in each subsequent quarterly meeting, set revenue and profit targets. You should also set a quarterly target for your key metric, which monitors your progress toward your Big Hairy Audacious Goal. Depending on the BHAG you've set, this may be the number of people impacted by your services, your market share, number of customers, revenue per employee, or something similar.

After setting your company's Rocks, make sure that team members also share their individual priorities for the quarter with each other. This will ensure that they aren't overcommitting to lesser initiatives at the expense of the company's Rocks. Sharing also allows you to uncover and agree on any interdependencies, and create clarity and transparency around who is doing what.

Act on Lead Measures

You just set your revenue, profit, and key metric targets for the quarter. These are "rearview mirror" indicators, or lag measures; to reach them, different parts of your business must perform key activities. For example, generating revenues requires you to bill for products or services that you have provided to your customers. Profit depends on your revenues and that you deliver your services cost efficiently and in sufficient quantities. Meeting your key metric, such as revenue per employee, requires your people to become more productive by working with increasing effectiveness and efficiency.

After updating your books at the end of the quarter, you will know whether you have achieved these objectives, but you cannot directly control them at that point.

Windshield Indicators. To ensure you track your plans, you need "windshield" indicators, or lead measures. Let's take a consulting business as an example.

Achieving your **revenue target** will require you to acquire new customers and deliver services to them on time. You may measure these by tracking the following areas:

- **Marketing activities**, such as social media posts, pieces of content created, and the number of attendees registered for your webinar to generate leads

117

- **Sales activities**, including the number of leads engaged through calls, meetings, and issuing proposals to convert leads into customers
- **Service capacity growth**, by tracking the number of consultants hired and onboarded, and the number of professional certifications obtained.

Profits are a result of revenues and the cost effectiveness of your operations, which you may measure by tracking

- **Gross margins** achieved by optimizing profitability by client and type of service,
- Administrative expense lines against budget to **reduce overhead**, and
- Number of days receivables outstanding to **reduce financing expenses**.

Your key metric of revenue per employee may be achieved by monitoring:

- The utilization of billable employees to ensure everyone is **generating revenue**
- Net promoter scores to track **client satisfaction**
- Employee engagement scores to measure the **organizational energy applied**
- Number of customer business review meetings to track **cross- and upselling efforts**

Your Rocks may not lend themselves to weekly measures, but you can often create milestones that can be tracked and ticked off during the quarter.

Keep a Compelling Scoreboard

The way to keep your people engaged is to gamify tracking your lead measures. Let them measure and hold each other accountable with the use of a scoreboard. "A players" love to keep score and are energized by knowing how they contribute, and they make sure everyone else is doing the same.

If you have identified your windshield indicators, measure them weekly on a scoreboard. Make sure every indicator has an owner who will report to the rest of the team whether they have hit their metric. Create a level playing field by making sure everyone on the team is accountable for metrics and no one is a bystander.

Each quarter, update the weekly goal. You may need 50 qualified leads to generate 20 calls, 10 meetings, and 5 proposals to yield 2 new clients a week, on average. You may need 85 percent utilization of your billable employees and 35 percent gross margin on closed engagements. You may have to keep your receivables at or below 30 days to have enough cash to pay your bills without tapping into your credit line. You might need to hire 13 employees each quarter to keep up with your growth plan, which is one a week.

Not every number on your scoreboard will be meaningful if you look at a week's results in isolation. You might convert seven new customers one week and have three dry weeks but still be on track with your plan. Use rolling averages to smooth out weekly variances at four weeks, 13 weeks (a calendar quarter), or maybe even 52 weeks for highly seasonal businesses. The pattern of your rolling average will tell you whether you are on track and still trending upward. If any of the metrics show a drift or even a slight decline, you know you must redouble your efforts to get your windshield number back on track.

Figure 6.4 Calculating a 6-Week Rolling Average

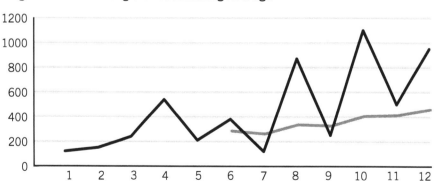

Source: "Moving Average," Excel Easy, https://www.excel-easy.com/examples/moving-average.html.

The Stumbling Scoreboarder. A contracting company I coached had a rocky start with scoreboarding. They quickly identified the key metrics they wanted to measure, but it soon became apparent that the information was hard to extract from their accounting system. After they figured that out, the ball dropped again when the person in charge of collecting the information was not held accountable. When they straightened out accountability, it turned out that they hit almost none of the numbers because they had picked targets that were too ambitious.

It took this client 12 months to master the scoreboard and hit half the numbers, and another six months to achieve 90 percent success in reaching their weekly targets. However long it took, they stuck with it. The business became highly profitable in their industry, he reined in their bloated working capital, and repaid the shareholder loans the owner had funded from his 401(k).

Make sure that your team is involved in creating your scoreboard and setting your Rocks. Encourage everyone to bring their ideas to the table each quarter to make sure your targets and priorities are co-created by the team for maximum buy-in. You as the leader can easily make sure that your ideas are in the mix and you sell your team on prioritizing them. Keep your mind and ears open to hear and incorporate your team's ideas as well.

Create a Cadence of Accountability

After your quarterly Rocks and your scoreboard are in place, the magic of execution happens by setting up a cadence of weekly team meetings. These meetings are an accountability tool that leverage the peer pressure of the group to get things done.

Achieving your Rocks and numbers becomes a habit, and you will need to work on your execution muscle. A typical team needs at least a couple of quarters to get decent at accomplishing Rocks and metrics; some need a couple of years. Others do extremely well in the first quarter, but then they burn themselves out. Make sure you pace yourself and build a sustainable effort.

Sandbagging Nonprofit. The most dysfunctional client I ever worked with was a nonprofit organization that accomplished 93 percent of their

Rocks in the first quarter we planned together. The results were impressive, until we discovered that they had selected business-as-usual items that only required a 40 percent effort to accomplish.

Let group members report to each other on hitting their weekly windshield numbers and Rocks, listing any off-track items to be discussed in priority order in the second part of that weekly meeting. A good practice is to spend 20–30 minutes on checking in on Rocks, discussing metrics with the leadership team, identifying issues and opportunities, and then spending a full hour solving issues and making decisions and assign action items as a result.

Make sure you don't use your weekly meeting for general discussion and status reports because it is easy to burn time with unstructured debate instead of making progress. The goal of your weekly meeting is to identify critical issues, discover root causes, harvest ideas from the team, make decisions, and get team members to commit to taking action. Make sure you follow up on your previous week's to-do items to confirm that they have been completed.

To solve issues, I suggest using a modified methodology of Vistage Worldwide, which goes as follows:

1. Prioritize your top issue.
2. Identify who "owns" it.
3. Have the owner frame the issue as a "How do I…" question.
4. Dig for the underlying reason by asking open-ended questions.
5. Restate the issue based on its root cause.
6. Ask another round of clarifying and probing questions.
7. Have participants make suggestions on how to solve the issue; make sure everyone feels heard.
8. Allow the leader to make a decision and support them.
9. Ensure the team member agrees to take action by the next weekly meeting.
10. If the action is bigger than a to-do, defer it to the next quarterly meeting. Slice off a one-week action to create momentum when a Rock-size problem needs your immediate attention.

Concept 6: Process

Entrepreneurial businesses often get stuck because the founder or the leadership team reaches their capacity. Delegating helps avoid getting to that point. However, delegating tasks that require knowledge, experience, or judgment is difficult. Straight delegation of complex responsibilities only works if your subordinates are knowledgeable and experienced. Such people are hard to find because any good employer protects and rewards them so that they stay put. Even if they occasionally become available, they will be expensive, requiring high salaries and/or equity incentives that may make hiring them prohibitive for a small business.

The answer is to design processes because processes enable you to delegate complex tasks to less-knowledgeable, less-experienced, or less-smart people. Green employees get it that they don't know enough; they are often starved for guidance but, they also hate to bother the busy boss about it. With processes in place, junior employees become a major resource for your business.

Unfortunately, most entrepreneurs shy away from working on processes. Their reticence often stems from fear, uncertainty, and misunderstanding surrounding the systemization of their business. They might fall victim to one of the following "process myths":

Processes Are Boring

In *The E-Myth* Michael Gerber talks about how most entrepreneurs start out as technicians: They were good at their job and figured they could do it more profitably for themselves. Others get into business to follow their passion for personal success, for making a difference, or for both. Few of us started a company because we loved processes. Frankly, processes may not feel like "visionary" work to you. Systemizing may sound mechanistic and repetitive rather than exciting. Besides, you might feel that there are more important things for you to do, such as hunting down new customers or cooking up solutions for the ones you already serve.

Processes Make You "Corporate"

You may feel that systemizing your business will deprive you of the fun of doing whatever you want in the moment, which may be why you struck out on your own in the first place. You'd hate to lose your freedom. What if having your business run on processes is soul-destroying, too? You don't want to turn your people into machines by having them labor on a conveyor belt, doing repetitive, noncreative work. Systemization may call to mind movies that depict square-jawed consultants in black suits reengineering processes to justify firings. You don't want that.

And what if systemizing your business kills your team's entrepreneurial spirit and makes your best people flee to nimbler competition? That would be terrible. It is your entrepreneurship that has helped you come this far.

Systemizing May Overwhelm

Just thinking about it gives you a headache. It is hard to visualize what the business would look like fully systemized. There are so many moving parts and you don't know where to even begin. Honestly, processes also sound complicated. They conjure up images of workflows, process charts with circles, diamonds, and arrows, and exhausting technology implementations. What if your systemizing project turned into a never-ending, costly distraction that you would ultimately be forced to abandon to save your business?

You Will Have to Let Go

And who can you trust to do the systemizing anyway? You fear that it may be beyond the pay grade of your inexperienced team. They have never done anything like that. What if they screw it up? It could turn into a terrible mess for you to clean up. Even if the systemizing worked, there could be bigger dangers ahead. What if the systems make people too lazy to think? What if a process is faulty and no one catches the mistake before customers get hurt or defects pile up? How will you control the beast that you have created? You may fear ending up with more fires than what you faced before you started systemizing.

Having to Enforce Processes Is Intimidating

Your biggest fear may be about sustaining the system. It is no good creating processes without being sure that you would be able to keep up the discipline and accountability required to maintain them. As for most visionary entrepreneurs, being consistent and systematic may not be your strong suit. You may also loathe tough conversations with people who are not delivering.

How about being wary of the resources you need to tie up to operate these processes? After all, it would require training people, measuring the frequency and quality of their execution, and ironing out any wrinkles that may arise when some procedures fail, as they are bound to do. Processes also need to be regularly updated, requiring the time and attention of your already stretched team. Who is going to do all that and how do you know that they would succeed?

But don't despair. Defining, documenting, simplifying, and following processes is much simpler than you think using Management Blueprint tools.

In *The E-Myth Revisited* Michael Gerber explains the three steps of creating processes, which he labels as the "Business Development Process"[54]:

1. **Innovation**: Identify your business's critical essentials from the perspective of your customers. Simplify your business and break it down into its critical essentials; Gerber calls this the "Best Way" skill.
2. **Quantification**: Measure the impact of how you deliver your Best Way to determine its value to the business. Translate your entire business to numbers so that you can measure what and how you do it.
3. **Orchestration**: Eliminate discretion and choice; in other words, document your proprietary Best Way to create a consistent experience.

Gerber's example is McDonald's, where every process has been codified and people are trained all over the world to deliver a consistent service quality and experience. In his follow-on work, *E-Myth Mastery,* Gerber illustrates processes as a linear chain of steps to be followed.[55]

Figure 6.5 How to Document Processes

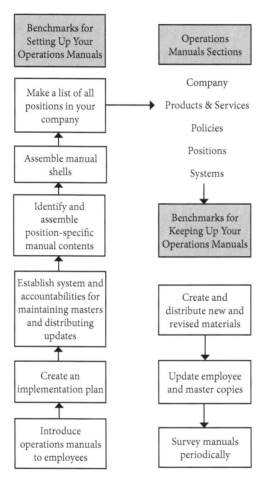

Source: Michael E. Gerber, *E-Myth Mastery*, p. 262.

Alternatively, you may use EOS's 3 Step Process Documenter™ tool to implement and roll out your core processes without breaking a sweat by identifying, simplifying, and documenting the key steps of your critical processes.

125

The three-person leadership team of Groove Commerce, a Baltimore-based e-commerce services company, decided to systemize their business. They identified nine core processes, including Sales, Marketing, HR, Finance, Production Management, Engagement, Products, Partnerships, and Client Satisfaction. Within six months, they implemented and rolled out all nine. Their people started to feel more productive and happier, and their profit margin went up 10 points because staff knew exactly what they should be doing and when, with minimal supervision. As their CEO Ethan Giffin told me at their mid-2020 quarterly meeting, "Our new hires were impressed with our onboarding process and client complaints all but disappeared in the middle of a pandemic."

Concept 7: Alignment

It takes, on average, two to three years for a company to master and ingrain a Management Blueprint at every level of its organization, but every company moves at its own pace.

The tool of alignment is to overcommunicate your vision. The best practice is to hold an all-hands meeting each quarter and walk your team through your core values, purpose or mission, BHAG, Vivid Vision, annual plan, and quarterly Rocks. It may take two years, but eventually your people will internalize your vision and fully commit to it. Those who do not resonate will sooner or later realize that they could not succeed in your company and they will leave. Good riddance.

The most languid adoption rate I have seen was by a 300-employee tech-enabled service company that started using EOS after a merger, with an 18-person leadership team. The organization took well over a year just to consolidate the team down to six people, who could then finally focus on strategic leadership and decision-making. The company-wide rollout of EOS sped up from that point. The most rapid business take-up was by an e-commerce system integrator that started weekly meetings at mid-management levels right out of the gate.

Running your business on a Management Blueprint allows you to keep breaking through ceilings until you have built the business to your target value and beyond. Operating using a Management Blueprint telegraphs to investors that you have a Buyable Business.

So, finally, you have a well-run organization that is self-managing, growing, and consistently profitable. But you are not done yet. In Part Three of this book, we will look into how to drive the value of the business higher by laying foundations for growth well in advance of a transaction, engineering value drivers into your business, and fine-tuning the company for a potential equity harvesting event.

KEY IDEAS

- This chapter gives you examples of how the Management Blueprints help you implement each of the Seven Management Concepts in your business.
- **Culture**: Jim Collins's Mission to Mars exercise helps you articulate your organization's core values, and Patrick Lencioni helps you build a cohesive organization.
- **Structure**: Michael Gerber helps you build clarity in your organization with position contracts, and Verne Harnish introduces the Function Accountability Chart that helps you understand the deliverables for each function and prioritize new hires.
- **Vision**: The three legs of your vision stool are Jim Collins's Purpose/Mission, BHAG, and Cameron Herold's medium-term Vivid Vision for your business.
- **Strategy**: The strategic toolkit, from Verne Harnish and Shannon Byrne Susko, includes analyzing your environment, formulating strategies using conceptual frameworks, setting annual goals, procuring resources, and monitoring and measuring implementation.
- **Execution**: The four disciplines of execution are setting a handful of wildly important goals, the quarterly Rocks; taking

action on lead measures; using a scoreboard to monitor them; and establishing a meeting cadence for accountability.

- **Process**: There are many reasons why entrepreneurs procrastinate on this critical tool. Follow Michael Gerber's trifecta of innovation, quantification, and orchestration, or use EOS's 3-Step Process Documenter to build your processes.
- **Alignment**: It takes two to three years to achieve alignment by overcommunicating your culture, vision, and plan to your employees.

TOOL FOR THE CHAPTER

Measure how well the management of your business is orchestrated at BuyabilityAssessment.com.

PART THREE:
DRIVE GROWTH AND VALUE

If you are this far into the book, you've come a long way. By now you should see clearly what Your Ideal Life could look like. You have your Magic Number and the current value of your business, and you have calculated the value you need to create in your business to fund the Next Chapter of your life, no matter whether it will take place inside or outside your company.

You have also started to orchestrate your business with EOS or another Management Blueprint. If you're using EOS, you have implemented a system that will strengthen the Six Key Components™ of your business so that within about two years it transforms into a well-oiled machine.

Now, a Management Blueprint may be all you need to get your business to the required value by your Next Chapter date, whether that is in 3 years or 10. In 2019, my clients who implemented EOS grew sales and profits on average by 22.1 percent and 27.5 percent, respectively. This translates to valuation growths of 25–30 percent per annum, or more, on average.

But there's no guarantee that using a Management Blueprint will grow your business by that degree. Or you might need to grow faster to reach your goals. It is also likely that making your business well-managed and healthy will not grow its value infinitely. You must pull other levers, too, at some point.

In the following three chapters, we explore three other such levers. Chapter 7 lays the foundation for your business so that you can eliminate major administrative obstacles to your company's buyability. Chapter 8 describes various business models and other value drivers that help you grow faster and more sustainably. Finally, in Chapter 9, we ensure your business is tidied up to show its best face to potential investors and buyers.

MASTER THE BASICS

Mastering the basics is all about removing impediments to the buyability of your business well in advance, so that you don't need to scramble when a buyer or investor appears on your doorstep. Such impediments typically involve one or more of the following:

- Not maintaining clean records and customers and vendors diversified
- Lack of sticky customers, who produce recurring revenues
- Failing to look after and protect your hard and intangible assets
- Not updating your contractual relationships so that they work for you, not against you

Now let's dive in and look at how to fix each of these in turn.

CLEAN RECORDS

Do you recall the Gulliver toy distribution company built by the ice hockey Hall of Fame friends? Gulliver was eminently buyable because the owners built it on a granite foundation. They made sure they were prepared and organized before they even knew they would ever sell the company. Gulliver would have scored an 8 or a 9 out of 10 on the buyability test. By following the principles discussed in Part Three of this book, you can do even better.

In Chapter 9, I talk about grooming a business for sale, when the business has matured into the asset that you need it to be. However, some steps take several years to implement without undue costs, and it is best to put the following building blocks in place early, while it is simple and risk free to do so.

Nothing discussed in this chapter is difficult or requires special expertise. You can do all this setup with some clear thinking and preparation. Just follow the recipe.

Keep Clean Books and Records

The secret to building a Buyable Business is to show outstanding potential for growth and profits and to eliminate all uncertainty and concern about the existing business.

Fear may be the strongest motivator but it is also an inhibitor of optimism. By working on eliminating uncertainty (fear of the unknown) for any potential buyers, you are at the same time building optimism about the business's potential future. Therefore, the most valuable step toward buyability is to build trust with the outside world.

Because financial statements are a window into the business, you can build tremendous trust by compiling clearly presented, consistent, and reliable financial statements.

Look, I started life as a KPMG accountant, so you can call me biased. But the fact is that most investors can read a balance sheet and do check financials first. Get these right and you will have taken an enormous step in the right direction.

So, how do you start down that road?

First, hire an inside or outside accountant and start recording your transactions. QuickBooks is an excellent tool, and you can start from there. Ask your accountant to be thorough in recording your business's expenses in the proper categories.

At the end of your first fully recorded year, analyze your revenues and expenses and create a budget for the next year. You can do that by projecting your revenues by major categories for the year and then breaking it down into quarters. Look at the seasonality of last year's revenues or guesstimate the percentages of your annual sales that fall into the individual quarters.

Next, look at your gross margin and decide whether you can increase it next year or maintain it. Let's say your sales revenue was $10 million and your gross profit (sales minus direct expenses) was $2.5 million, giving you a 25 percent gross margin. If you increase your revenues to $11 million, will you keep the same gross margin or increase it to, say, 27 percent? What would it take to increase the margin?

If you know your gross profit, review each of last year's selling, general, and administrative expense (SG&A) items and calculate them as a percentage of sales. Some of these expenses, such as sales commissions, will probably increase in line with sales, some will increase with inflation, and others will increase with inflation plus or minus a few percent points.

This simple method will give you a next-year budget. From there, record your numbers diligently each month and review your revenue, gross profit margin, and net profit margin figures each month—and try to beat your annual projections.

You will soon find that your understanding of your numbers grows. You will be able to build a more reliable budget and start breaking it down into a monthly plan much easier with experience and historical numbers. (See Table 7.1.)

Table 7.1 Simple Annual Budget with Analysis

		Last year actual					Next year budget				
INSULATION & FOUNDATION CONSTRUCTION, INC.		Q1	Q2	Q3	Q4	20XX Actual	Q1	Q2	Q3	Q4	20XY Budget
Income											
	Insulation Income	132.6	38.5	188.3	166.5	525.9	242.0	254.1	292.2	306.8	1,094.9
	% of Total Income	27.2%	7.6%	22.9%	19.8%	19.8%	25.0%	25.0%	25.0%	25.0%	25.0%
	Foundation Income	354.5	470.8	632.9	675.1	2,133.2	725.9	762.2	876.5	920.3	3,284.8
	% of Total Income	72.8%	92.4%	77.1%	80.2%	80.2%	75.0%	75.0%	75.0%	75.0%	75.0%
Total Income		487.1	509.3	821.2	841.6	2,659.1	967.8	1,016.2	1,168.6	1,227.1	4,379.7
Income growth per quarter/year			4.6%	61.2%	2.5%		15.0%	5.0%	15.0%	5.0%	64.7%
Cost of Goods Sold											
	COGS - Insulation	22.1	6.2	41.0	24.7	94.0	43.3	45.4	52.2	54.8	195.7
	% of Insulation Income	16.7%	16.1%	21.8%	14.8%	17.9%	17.9%	17.9%	17.9%	17.9%	108.2%
	COGS - Foundation	195.3	260.4	363.9	381.7	1,201.3	408.8	429.2	493.6	518.3	1,849.8
	% of Foundation Income	55.1%	55.3%	57.5%	56.5%	56.3%	56.3%	56.3%	56.3%	56.3%	54.0%
	Wages - Insulation	9.5	11.8	35.4	34.5	91.1	41.9	44.0	50.6	53.2	189.8
	% of Insulation Income	7.2%	30.6%	18.8%	20.7%	17.3%	17.3%	17.3%	17.3%	17.3%	17.3%
	Wages - Foundation	21.7	55.2	55.5	78.2	210.8	71.7	75.2	86.5	90.9	324.3
	% of Foundation Income	6.1%	11.7%	8.8%	11.6%	9.9%	9.9%	9.9%	9.9%	9.9%	9.9%
Total COGS		248.6	333.6	495.8	519.1	1,597.0	565.6	593.9	683.0	717.1	2,559.6
Gross Profit		238.5	175.7	325.3	322.5	1,062.0	402.2	422.3	485.7	509.9	1,820.1
Gross Profit Margin		49.0%	34.5%	39.6%	38.3%	39.9%	41.6%	41.6%	41.6%	41.6%	41.6%
SG&A Expenses											
	Salaries	73.2	85.4	110.4	125.1	394.1	123.1	123.1	123.1	123.1	492.6
	% of Total Income	15.0%	16.8%	13.4%	14.9%	14.8%	12.7%	12.1%	10.5%	10.0%	11.2%
	Insurance Expense	10.5	2.2	17.2	3.5	33.4	12.1	12.8	14.7	15.4	55.0
	% of Total Income	2.2%	0.4%	2.1%	0.4%	1.3%	1.3%	1.3%	1.3%	1.3%	1.3%
	Professional Fees	5.2	7.7	12.7	10.1	35.7	10.6	11.2	12.9	13.5	48.2
	% of Total Income	1.1%	1.5%	1.5%	1.2%	1.3%	1.1%	1.1%	1.1%	1.1%	1.1%
	Advertising	2.8	7.1	4.3	3.3	17.5	8.7	9.1	10.5	11.0	39.4
	% of Total Income	0.6%	1.4%	0.5%	0.4%	0.7%	0.9%	0.9%	0.9%	0.9%	0.9%
	Rent Expense	0.8	3.0	3.0	6.8	13.6	3.6	3.6	3.6	3.6	14.3
	% of Total Income	0.2%	0.6%	0.4%	0.8%	0.5%	0.4%	0.4%	0.3%	0.3%	0.3%
	Payroll and Benefits	8.3	10.2	13.5	15.5	47.5	14.8	14.8	14.8	14.8	59.4
	% of Salaries	11.3%	11.9%	12.2%	12.4%	12.1%	12.1%	12.1%	12.1%	12.1%	12.1%
	Other SG&A Expenses	15.0	16.3	23.7	26.1	81.1	29.0	30.5	35.1	36.8	131.4
	% of Total Income	3.1%	3.2%	2.9%	3.1%	3.0%	3.0%	3.0%	3.0%	3.0%	3.0%
Total SG&A Expenses		115.7	131.9	184.8	190.5	622.9	202.1	205.1	214.7	218.3	840.2
Net Profit		122.8	43.8	140.6	132.0	439.1	200.1	217.2	271.0	291.6	979.9
Net Profit Margin		25.2%	8.6%	17.1%	15.7%	16.5%	20.7%	21.4%	23.2%	23.8%	22.4%

134

It isn't enough to have your accountant prepare annual financial statements. You need to have a budgeting and review process inside your company. Build your own and your team's muscles for creating and following budgets and plans.

If you can afford it, use an auditor to review and validate your financial statements, and ask this person to provide a management letter that offers feedback on where you can improve. Within two or three years, you will have a set of consistent, clean financial statements and budgets that are more accurate every year. You will understand your financial flows and position, which will put you in a much better place to control profitability.

STRUCTURE CUSTOMERS

You don't just want to take any customer you can get. You want to sell to customers who you can satisfy, sell to at the right price and on the right terms, and preferably sell to repeatedly. In the words of marketing guru Dan Kennedy, "Don't get a customer to make a sale, make a sale to get a customer." The structure of your revenues and the diversity of your customers directly influence the buyability of your business.

Recurring Revenues and Long-Term Contracts

The value of your business chiefly depends on the cash flows it generates into the future. However, the future is uncertain, so how do you convince others that those cash flows will come?

Buyers and investors fret over one-off contracts because they fear the churn of customers after they have taken over the business. This uncertainty is reflected in how they value companies. Project-driven businesses, such as construction and consulting firms, often attract EBITDA multiples as low as two to three times, whereas wealth management companies with "perpetual" customers often sell for seven to nine times EBITDA.

That is why investors look for companies that have long-term contracts, or at least recurring revenues. What magic when you sell a customer once and they stay for a long time! With a history of "sticky" customers like this, your business will be valued at a much higher multiple of cash flows than if you have to find new customers every year. Unfortunately, my business, MB Partners, did not have sticky customers. We helped our clients sell their business, so if we did our job, they ceased being our customers. This fact made MB Partners dependent on bringing in new clients all the time, which made it harder to generate revenues.

Optimal Networks, the IT service company mentioned earlier, recently switched from charging for on-site service to a flat pricing model. The switch was scary because Optimal could have made a loss by overservicing clients that presented operational challenges or had unreasonable expectations, but the company soon found the right price point and service level. Its clients were happy because their IT spends became more predictable and their MSP now had a built-in incentive to work precisely, fast, and without errors. Optimal also became more profitable.

SaaS companies attract even higher multiples if they keep their churn low. A SaaS company I know that provides cybersecurity solutions to large corporations is aiming to reach $16 million in annual recurring revenue by the end of the fiscal year. Its Vivid Vision is to get to $35 million in three years. This means it must continue to improve its software, provide great customer service, and find new customers. When it reaches critical size, where it is fast-growing and has low churn (loss of customers), investors may value it at 5 to 10 times its annual revenues.[56]

Compare this to the valuation of similar-sized generic software businesses at 7 to 10 times EBITDA, even though these companies also have service revenues that recur.[57] When clients commit to not just a service provider but also a technology solution, their stickiness increases further, and the business attracts an even higher multiple of earnings.

In the book *The Automatic Customer*, John Warrillow describes six recurring revenue models in order of increasing stickiness: consumables revenue, sunk money consumables revenue, subscription revenue, sunk money subscription revenue, perpetual subscription revenue, and contract revenue.[58] (See Figure 7.2.)

Figure 7.2 Warrillow's Six Types of Recurring Revenues

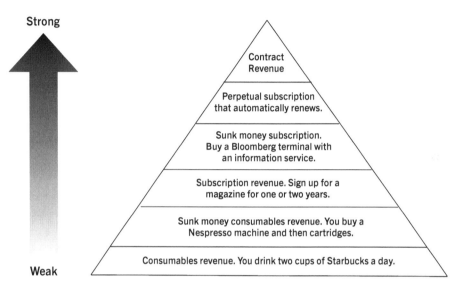

Always ponder how you can make your customers sticky. One strategy is to make yourself indispensable to them so they won't consider leaving. The second step is to structure transactions into convenient services with a perpetual subscription. This is how Chris Grandpre built Mosquito Squad, where customers pay a monthly fee for solving the "bug problem" forever. Provided the service works and is affordable, there is no reason to ever cancel it.

The longer your clients are willing to commit to you, the more stability and value your business has in the eyes of investors. Think about how you can make yourself more trusted and indispensable to your customers so that it increases the switching cost of replacing you and they stick instead.

Diversify Customers and Vendors

A business's exposure to the loss of a single customer or vendor when it has few can be perilous. These counterparts—clients and suppliers—are outside of your business, so you have no control over them. If they mess up or lose confidence in you, they can walk away, putting your business at risk if you rely on just a small number.

Held Hostage by a Big Customer

An organizational culture consulting firm I call Lewis & Clark, Inc. (L&C) exploded on the back of insatiable demand from a large consumer products company, Feldue. After initial setbacks, the two partners of L&C built a $5 million sales revenue company by servicing Feldue and other companies that found them mainly through word of mouth.

There was one catch, however: More than 70 percent of L&C's revenues came from Feldue, and Feldue's demand for L&C's corporate services kept increasing. The consulting firm was under pressure to hire and staff Feldue projects, with little capacity left for landing other clients. It was in mortal danger of losing Feldue, which would put it out of business. This led the L&C team to walk on eggshells around their biggest customer and to take on projects that were bad fits for their firm.

L&C tried to diversify, but Feldue kept it busy, and handcuffed. Eventually, the two founders had a falling out and parted ways, and L&C started sliding backward. It is now down from more than 40 employees to 10 and is no longer the Buyable Business its founders wanted to build.

Customer Concentration Making you Untouchable

Another business I'll call Computa, a data-mining company, built up a thriving business supplying custom software solutions to the energy sector. It generated more than $40 million in sales and a respectable 10 percent EBITDA margin.

The two owners of the business, Drew and Jason, hired us to find a buyer for the company. We canvassed the market and got more than a hundred interested buyers to sign nondisclosure agreements. We expected a swift, competitive sale at an EBITDA multiple of six to seven times. Computa's profit margin was average, but the data-mining industry was heating up, and Computa had some recurring revenues.

Computa's biggest client was the Siemens group, which at one point represented 90 percent of Computa's sales revenues. Siemens was not a single customer. Computa worked with separate legal entities across 15 countries, and over 20 years had built up more than 2,000 contacts in the global Siemens organization.

Nevertheless, notwithstanding the diversification within Siemens, this was a major turnoff for Computa's suitors: 97 percent of the interested parties withdrew, and Computa received only three offers that priced the business at a lowly two to three times EBITDA, less than half of what we and our clients had hoped. Drew and Jason postponed their retirement plans and turned the company into an ESOP to facilitate their exit plans. As you can see from Computa's example, not just actual concentration but even the perception of concentration can easily destroy the buyability of your business.

Lethal Vendor Concentration

In the early 2000s, I followed Rába, a public automotive company that produced axles for agricultural vehicles for US and Canadian original equipment manufacturers and car seats and other components for Suzuki and other Central European car plants.

After the 2001 recession, and loss of orders from its major OEM customers, Rába cut costs and renegotiated vendor contracts. Its vehicle seat division was the dominant supplier for Suzuki's compact city car the Swift, and Rába used its position to force price rises with its major customer.

Suzuki grudgingly went along, as it had no immediate alternative. It kept models for six years, so it could amortize its development and equipment investments. However, it retaliated by developing two alternative suppliers for its next model and withdrawing half its business from Rába two years later. Suzuki learned its lesson and stopped relying on a single supplier for any of its car parts in Central Europe.

As Dan Kennedy used to say: "The worst number in business is one." One vendor, one salesperson, one IT expert. Your business needs to stand on multiple legs and diversify away its dependence on individual customers, vendors, and employees.

MANAGE ASSETS

After making sure your most important assets—your customers—are in order, don't forget to look after your physical assets, too. They are part of your business and will influence its buyability as well as its value and what you can keep of it after paying the tax collector.

Update Your Technology and Equipment

Andrew, a veteran of the prefabricated concrete industry, founded an entrepreneurial business manufacturing slabs, pillars, and other building components. He built the business from scratch on the site of a former military installation by buying used equipment from bankrupt competitors. He was an honest businessman and a magnetic salesperson and grew the venture to number four in his geographical market behind three international groups.

Andrew promised his wife he'd retire so they could travel, and in 2007, as the economy was booming, he asked us to find a buyer for his business. The financial performance, the business plan, and the management team intrigued a French construction group, which made an attractive offer. We were excited and expected no major obstacles to signing an LOI and moving forward with the deal.

Unfortunately, this was not to be. The buyer from the French group was shocked when he saw the production equipment for pouring concrete into molds in all seasons set up in an open-air facility. The company was producing good-quality products and had robust equipment. But to an executive of an international concern, who was used to indoor facilities and clean conditions, this was an alien approach. He cut the meeting short, skipped lunch, and caught an early flight back to Paris.

Had the equipment been newer and better presented, the deal would have almost certainly closed. Another former client, a civil construction firm, made it company policy to replace all vehicles and production equipment within four years of purchase. Leadership figured this was the optimal period to use their machines if they were to minimize maintenance costs and optimize work efficiency, company image, and client satisfaction.

Be strategic about managing and replacing equipment so that your business is perceived as current and invulnerable.

Set Up a Tax-Efficient Business Structure

First off, I am not a tax advisor, so please make sure you have up-to-date professional support. What I do know is that you can save a lot of money by having the right tax framework set up for your business well in advance of doing a sale, recapitalization, or other transaction.

In the United States
BNY Mellon Wealth Management discusses three groups of tax strategies to reduce the tax burden on building, operating, and transitioning small businesses.[59]

Estate freezing and transfer techniques allow business owners to transfer highly appreciating assets to their kids, deferring capital gains taxes and avoiding paying tax on gifts and inheritances. These strategies include the following:

- Annual gifting
- Installment sales to an intentionally defective grantor trust
- Private annuities
- Grantor-retained annuity trusts

Rollovers, exclusions, and tax deferral techniques allow business owners to use certain sections of the tax code by entering into a transaction or creating special legal entities. These include

- Section 1042 to sell stock to an ESOP and roll over the proceeds into qualified replacement property, where taxes can be deferred and extinguished on death
- Section 1202 Capital Gains Exclusion of up to 50 percent on qualified small business stock (QSBS) held for five years or longer
- Section 1045 rollover, allowing the taxable gains from one QSBS to be transferred to another
- Section 1045 rollover combined with Section 1202, to keep some sale proceeds as cash

Special deductions and state income tax avoidance strategies allow business owners to set up the following transfers:

- Interest charge domestic international sales corporations to convert ordinary income into qualified dividend income
- Incomplete gift non-grantor trusts to shift assets from high-tax states such as California and New Jersey to low-tax jurisdictions such as Nevada and Delaware and to avoid state capital gains

In the European Union

In the EU, the Merger Directive allows for the tax-free cross-border reorganization of companies, and entrepreneurs have created holding companies in low-tax jurisdictions, such as Cyprus and Ireland. You can do this free of capital gains tax by swapping the shares of an operating company to that of the holding entity. After the transaction, the entrepreneur owns the stock of the holding and the holding owns the former operating business. Upon the sale of the operating business, the proceeds go to the holding, which can reinvest that money tax deferred.[60]

European small business owners routinely set up such holding companies and transfer their assets to them before the sale. It is important, however, to prove that the reorganization is real and the tax optimization is just one of multiple reasons for setting up the structure. It is worth getting tax advice at least two years before a sale to minimize the risk of the authorities reclassifying the transaction to a taxable one.

These are just a handful of tax strategies that are worth investigating—the earlier the better—if you ever want to exit or transition your business.

Some business owners don't start the tax structuring early enough to save costs. Then they have to scramble in the eleventh hour, sometimes transferring their properties weeks or days before a transaction, which poses the risk of being penalized with taxes.

Even if you contemplate a future of no transactions, you can protect your assets against litigation or judgments by setting up a separate limited liability company (LLC) in an asset-protection-friendly state and potentially a domestic or foreign asset protection trust to transfer your assets into, with the help of your wealth manager and specialist tax advisors.[61]

Review your business structure at least two or three years before a potential transaction so that you can optimize it for your most likely financial plan without having to take excessive legal or tax risks to implement these changes.

UPDATE CONTRACTS

Make sure your contracts are written the right way so that you avoid unpleasant surprises that can derail your buyability later. These are easy fixes when done early, even without a potential sale in sight, but they can be awkward, expensive, and often impossible when you're close to an ownership transition.

Rethink Shareholder Agreements

Having business continuity agreements in place with your fellow stock-holders provides another block in a solid foundation. As partnerships grow, the balance between partners can shift, and not having a mechanism to resolve disputes can paralyze your business.

Last year a West Virginia–based insulation contractor, Douglas, approached me and asked my advice about a partnership dispute he was having with his cofounder, Nick. They had started the company as equal partners some years earlier, but their relationship had deteriorated. In the beginning they served customers side by side, but as the business grew, Douglas took on most of the management, sales, and financial responsibilities, while Nick remained just a technician. They both continued to draw small salaries and shared profits equally, an arrangement that less and less reflected their unique contributions. Douglas was also frustrated about having to wait for Nick's input into decisions he would eventually have to make himself anyway. It just caused unnecessary delays.

Nick resented Douglas's faster evolution, felt insecure about losing status in front of employees, and insisted on maintaining the status quo as 50–50 shareholders. After mediation failed, I suggested Douglas develop a BATNA—his best alternative to a negotiated agreement—sit down with Nick, and propose buying out some of Nick's shares.

Douglas's BATNA was to walk away and set up a competing business with his brother, because he had no noncompete agreement with Nick. Upon deciding to leave the business if they could not agree, Douglas attempted to negotiate a partial buyout and CEO rights for himself, while Nick would remain a substantial shareholder in a prospering and fast-growing business. It turned out to be a win-win, and Nick agreed to the buyout. But still, there was no guarantee in place that the issue would not resurface if Nick's proportionate contribution continued to slide.

In another instance, the 50–50 owners of an HVAC contractor could not renegotiate their partnership and ended up splitting the business in two and going their separate ways. They both ended up losing, having to rebuild their respective organizations and create duplicate support functions that depleted profits in both successor businesses.

The message is this: You should address such partnership tensions as soon as possible, because the longer you allow them to fester, the more difficult they become to resolve. If you are building a valuable asset and you and your partner are not seeing eye to eye, it's best for you to develop a BATNA and confront the situation.

A friend of mine, Benjamin, had a 23 percent stake in a spice production company he had cofounded with his former boss. Their relationship worked for a few years, but over time Benjamin became the dominant value driver of the business. He tried but was unable to renegotiate the relationship and ended up leaving to set up his own business. That venture was profitable from day one, and Benjamin could afford to pay himself a salary comparable to what he was earning in the partnership setup. Unfortunately, his former partner mishandled the original business to the point of ruin, and they both lost the equity they had built up in their partnership.

Find a specialist attorney to help you create a shareholders' agreement that includes mechanisms that enable you to negotiate changes over time, including rules and valuation guidelines that govern a potential sale, buyout, or capital raising.

Noncompetes and Confidentiality

Make sure that as your employees grow in stature, you negotiate noncompetes with them so they cannot hurt your business in the event of a sale and cannot share trade secrets or jump aboard a competitor. Setting up noncompete agreements is impossible or risky when a transaction is already in motion, but you can easily make them earlier, linking them to a promotion or a raise.

Also, be sure your suppliers are supporting you and keeping your trade secrets confidential. You don't want to be at their mercy when an acquirer requests their reassurance as a condition of buying your business.

KEY IDEAS

- Be methodical about building a solid foundation for your business by removing any structural impediments to its buyability. Be aware that certain foundation-building techniques take time to implement or must be carried out well in advance of a sale or capital transaction.
- Make sure you keep consistent and reliable financial statements that present a transparent and gradually improving financial picture of your business. Learn to build and track a simple budget in Excel. With it, you can project your cash flow and make changes in good time, as necessary, to avoid losses.
- Focus on building recurring revenue models by making yourself indispensable to your customers. Companies with recurring revenues are several times more valuable, not to mention more buyable, than others that have to originate new customers and projects continually.
- Make sure you don't depend on any individual customer or vendor. Keep each below 10 percent of your revenue. Your goal is to be able to weather the loss of any customer or vendor without a major disruption in business.
- Be strategic about your equipment purchases. Make sure your business is perceived as up-to-date and invulnerable.
- Set up a corporate structure that is tax efficient and protects you from predatory litigation.
- Review and update your shareholder agreements and noncompetes to minimize disputes and the risk of losing key employees when you're negotiating a sale or capital transaction.
- Building the foundation doesn't take special expertise, just time, some expense, and discipline, all of which pay back big later.

8

ENGINEER VALUE

Wealth is created from creating value.

—RANDY GAGE

A friend of mine, Chris Grandpre, owns Outdoor Living Brands, a collection of franchised businesses connected to activities around residential homes. These businesses include companies that build outside leisure and entertainment areas, maintain the lighting in buildings, and provide irrigation services. Several years ago, Chris acquired a young start-up residential and commercial company called Mosquito Squad that helped property owners prevent mosquitoes and other insects from taking over the yard and making outdoor living uncomfortable.

Chris had already owned four different franchise brands, all of which he had acquired and each of which had its own challenges in turning it into a scalable and Buyable Business. When repositioning Mosquito Squad, he wanted to build buyability into it by intentionally redesigning it to appeal to potential buyers. Because the core service involved packaging a repeatable, trainable consumer service into a product, he followed the recipe laid out in *Built to Sell*, by John Warrillow.[62]

According to Warrillow, investors love consumer businesses with the following characteristics:

They involve an evergreen service. Preventing mosquitoes and insects is an ongoing process and can be delivered with an ongoing contract that clients buy once and use as long as they need the results, potentially "forever."

They are not at the mercy of any customer. Bug prevention is a reasonably low-price-point service, affordable by millions of middle-class households. Losing individual clients doesn't threaten the business.

The business is run on processes, from sales to production. The Mosquito Squad process was a simple service that hourly employees could perform when trained. The service also doesn't need sophisticated salespeople, just good local marketing that can be cookie cutter.

They make the owner irrelevant. Chris hired a president from the get-go to run the day-to-day while he operated as a visionary leader who focused on marketing and scaling strategies.

They don't tie up cash in receivables or inventories. Chris charged annually up front for the service, which allowed him to scale using customer funds. He also had no sellable product to store, only limited inventories of the insecticides used in the business. This strategy is designed to avoid the fate of companies, such as those in earlier examples, that have to borrow from banks to finance inventories and receivables.

They ignore opportunities outside their core focus. Mosquito Squad succeeded in avoiding shiny objects and stayed in its lane, specializing in mosquito and insect abatement. Chris knew he had to stay focused, even if he became bored with the business, which sometimes happens when processes are fully repeatable and systemized.

Eight years later one of Chris's investors was looking to exit the group, so Chris tested the market for investment capital that would fund a buyout of those who wished to exit. The market's reactions surprised him. Mosquito Squad was valued by far the most highly, as it ticked all the boxes that investors were looking for: It was self-managing, and it had recurring revenue and sticky contracts. The business ran on simple processes that new employees could be trained in in days. It had a marketing engine that drove leads and brought on new franchisees regularly. The business was scalable in other geographies without management bottlenecks.

Chris pivoted and instead of a capital raise at the group level, he sold 100 percent of the bug elimination company and used the proceeds to buy out all his partners and become the controlling owner of the franchise management group.

By systematically engineering value drivers into his business, Chris turned a small mom-and-pop business into the most valuable piece of his portfolio.

VALUE DRIVERS

What drives value?

Professional investors consider two types of drivers: those that arise from operational synergies between the acquirer and the buyable target and those inherent in a Buyable Business.

Operational Synergies

Operational synergies are value enhancements created when an acquired business is integrated into an acquirer's existing operations or when the two businesses are directed in a coordinated fashion.

Broadly speaking, operational synergies may save costs or enhance revenues. Cost synergies are more predictable and controllable. The merger of consolidating industries such as banking and utilities are typically driven by cost savings. Their goal is to minimize the loss of customers, combine back offices to eliminate duplicated functions, and lay off employees. Becoming larger often increases pricing power, allowing cheaper procurement.

Growth synergies are more difficult to harvest because they require seamless cooperation of the acquirer and acquiree in cross selling each other's products or services or in combining each other's skills.[63] This is often hampered by the slow migration of systems and cultural differences between the two companies and ill feelings by the employees of the party (often the acquiree) that suffers the lion's share of the layoffs.

Synergies may drive value to the extent that you see what your typical buyers are looking for and mold your company into a desired target. When your business represents synergistic opportunities and you have multiple suitors, you may be able to capture some of that synergy value through negotiating a higher purchase price.

Inherent Value Drivers

In essence, investors want to buy the future cash flows of a business at a discount. This means they wish to acquire companies they believe will grow cash flows substantially, predictably, and sustainably into the future. All that without requiring "babysitting" by the buyer or causing the buyer headaches. The more stable the underlying technology, business model, company management, industry, product or service, customers, vendors, and economic environment, the better.

So, how can you engineer these traits into a business? I group the major value drivers into three categories: (1) Finding a Blue Ocean, (2) Pulling Out the Stops, and (3) Fine-Tuning the Machine.

Now, let's peel the onion on each of these.

FIND A BLUE OCEAN

W. Chan Kim and Renée Mauborgne coined the concept of the Blue Ocean Strategy in their book of the same title.[64] They make the case that you should look for "blue oceans" with minimal competition to get away from the commodity markets, or shark-infested, bloody "red oceans."

In this section, we will discuss three strategies for finding blue oceans.

Pivot to an Expanding Market

Investors are always looking to buy businesses that provide products or services for which demand is increasing. This puts the wind in their sails so that their portfolio companies can grow and gain profitability without major strategic shifts. Businesses in shrinking markets are vulnerable and require risky strategic moves to maintain, let alone create value for their shareholders.

Figures 8.1 and 8.2 show the least and most attractive sectors to invest in, according to the US Bureau of Labor Statistics.[65]

Figure 8.1 Industries to Avoid: The 10 Fastest-Declining Industries in the US in 2019

	Industry	2019-2020 Revenue Growth
1	Wind Turbine Manufacturing	-42.1%
2	Indoor Climbing Walls	-26.1%
3	Department Stores	-26.0%
4	Gasoline & Petroleum Bulk Stations	-23.9%
5	Sign & Banner Manufacturing Franchises	-21.2%
6	Petroleum Refining	-21.0%
7	Used Car Dealers	-18.7%
8	Oil Drilling & Gas Extraction	-18.0%
9	Media Representation Firms	-15.1%
10	Metal Tank Manufacturing	-14.1%

Source: "Industries with the Fastest Growing and Most Rapidly Declining Wage and Salary Employment," US Bureau of Labor Statistics, last modified September 1, 2020, https://www.bls.gov/emp/tables/industries-fast-grow-decline-employment.htm.

Figure 8.2 Industries to Target: The 10 Fastest-Growing Industries in the US

	Industry	2019-2020 Revenue Growth
1	3-D Printing & Rapid Prototyping Services	28.8%
2	Hydraulic Fracturing Services	27.8%
3	Autonomous Underwater Vehicle Manufacturing	26.7%
4	Medical & Recreational Marijuana Growing	25.2%
5	Medical & Recreational Marijuana Stores	23.4%
6	Video Conferencing Software Developers	21.4%
7	Hand Sanitizer Manufacturing	18.7%
8	Massage Franchises	18.0%
9	3-D Printer Manufacturing	17.9%
10	Personal Protective Equipment Manufacturing	17.4%

Source: "Industries with the Fastest Growing and Most Rapidly Declining Wage and Salary Employment," US Bureau of Labor Statistics, last modified September 1, 2020, https://www.bls.gov/emp/tables/industries-fast-grow-decline-employment.htm.

Substantial growth is much likelier to occur in growing industries, where it is enough for a business to grow with the market and there is less pressure for the firm to take market share from others. When you are operating in a growing sector, you have a lot more margin for error. In a shrinking market, you have to run twice as hard to cover the same distance.

So, how do you know if your market is declining?

The most obvious sign is falling revenue, which often leads to excess capacities and inventories. Some of your competitors are going bankrupt or exiting the market, but their production assets are picked up by others on the cheap, so capacity doesn't necessarily disappear. The extra capacity and inventory lead to price competition and compressing profit margins.

Even in a shrinking market you can employ strategies to survive—and sometimes to thrive long term—until you can pivot:[66]

Harvesting Your Mature Business Line

Take the profits that are available without investing in people, technology, or production equipment. The harvest time can be used to build up your new business so you can pivot upon reaching your inflection point. You reach this point when your existing business has become too onerous to sustain or when your predominant income potential has shifted to your new business line.

I have used this strategy multiple times. When going from M&A advisory to executive coaching, I stopped going after new investment business and harvested my existing portfolio of clients for income while I built my Vistage CEO peer groups. I did the same when I exited from Vistage and started my EOS implementation practice. The harvest and pivot is a great strategy for continually replacing parts of your business with higher-profit and higher-potential services.

Aiming to Become the Profitable Survivor

This strategy is for the player who has superior knowledge of the industry and can anticipate a sustainable future state when the market will stabilize. The survivor's goal is to manage the business's cost structure by acquiring failing competitors and leveraging economies of scale. The risk of this strategy is that the market keeps falling through the expected floor.

This happened to the public payphones market, which kept shrinking until it disappeared completely. One of my former clients, who bought out a direct mail printing business, suffered the same fate when digital marketing continued to erode his market. One day he disappeared without a trace and his employees found themselves locked out of the building. I assume he got out with whatever he could salvage.

Developing a niche strategy

Even in niche markets some pockets stay vibrant. Your business can thrive and grow if you can serve that niche really well. The vinyl record market has been shrinking for decades, but there is a niche audience that wants everything on vinyl, and few companies serve them.

Whether you're in a growing or a declining market, find a way to grow your share. Of two businesses with the same revenues and profit margins, the one with the larger market share is more valuable because it is more in control of defending its position. The larger your market share, the more you can dictate pricing and fight off competitors. Market leaders often receive better prices from suppliers, which helps them maintain healthier margins than rivals.

Pick Sustainable Technologies

No marketing, no sales engine, not even customer service can protect a business when a disrupting technology emerges. It took Zoom weeks to disrupt the conference and seminar industry when COVID-19 hit in early March 2020.

Creative destruction is the life force of economic growth, but it is painful to be on the receiving end. So, when buying a company, investors keep their sensitive antennas tuned to any signal of potential technological or business model disruption.

Disrupting technologies are like smartphones and their accompanying app business model, which disrupted laptops as the primary way consumers use the Internet. Cell phone cameras have disrupted the photography market and redefined what it means to take a photo and who has access to this technology.

Some industries being disrupted in 2020 include these:

- Travel websites shrink the need for human travel agents
- Tax software such as TurboTax eliminate jobs for tax accountants
- Online language translation, dictation, and proofreading services reduce the needs for human service providers
- Software and mobile apps are replacing secretaries and executive assistants
- Online bookstores and e-books replaced brick-and-mortar booksellers

- Checks can be deposited via mobile apps or at automated teller machines, reducing the need for human bank tellers
- LinkedIn, Indeed.com, and Monster are replacing job recruiters
- Uber, Lyft, and other car-sharing apps crowd out traditional taxi and livery companies
- Airbnb and HomeAway are doing the same in the hotel and motel industry
- Drone technology is revolutionizing product delivery and will replace some pilots
- 3-D printing is disrupting manufacturing, logistics, and inventory management
- Fast-food workers are being replaced by order-taking kiosks and self-checkout machines
- Instead of radio DJs, software chooses the music, inserts ads, and reads the news
- Online courses by leading universities are reducing the need for college professors

Although future disruptions are impossible to predict, keep your eyes open at all times so you can react quickly when your technology is becoming endangered. Disruptions rise like a tide, and you can change directions if you spot the trend early. Alternatively, take control of your destiny by seeking to become the disruptor yourself.

Find a Stable Business Model

So, let's look at some of the business models that are doing the disrupting or that appear stabilizing for the foreseeable future.

A business model describes the rationale of how an organization creates, delivers, and captures value. The process of constructing and modifying the business model is part of business strategy.

Investors look for companies whose business model is unlikely to be disrupted, that is, companies that will not be easily out-innovated by typically lower-priced competitors who expand to "disrupt" the premium segment.

Disrupting Business Models

What are the latest disrupting models that could come after your business?

A leading example is the "**freemium**" business model, used by such companies as Spotify and LinkedIn: The consumer receives a free product or service that is attractive, but not perfectly satisfying, so they pay for the premium version, which has all the desired features. This model works for products or services for which adding customers has low marginal cost and where marketing and customer information have a higher value than the operating costs.

Another model is to offer products and services as **subscriptions**, such as Netflix does. The consumer benefits by enjoying instant access to a service that otherwise would require a major capital investment, in return for entering a contractual relationship with the provider. The seller tries to retain the customer by constantly innovating and extending the service. Amazon started Prime as a free shopping subscription and later extended it into free and paid music and video-on-demand offerings.

Digital **marketplaces** that connect sellers and buyers on a common platform is another disruptive business model. The marketplaces make money via brokerage fees, membership fees, and advertising fees. eBay and Uber are good examples.

Exceptional customer experience adds value to an exchangeable product. Apple and Tesla embody this business model.

The **on-demand** model sells immediate access to people who have more time than money for people who have more money than time. Uber's driving services and Upwork's freelancers operate under this business model.

Some companies use **multiple disrupting models**. Uber and Amazon are both marketplaces and offer on-demand services at the same time.

Accenture's Disruptability Study

Accenture, a professional services company, analyzed 3,269 businesses—across 20 industries and 98 industry segments—for their susceptibility to disruption and then presented the results in the chart shown in Figure 8.3, where the vertical axis represents the current level of disruption in the industry and the horizontal axis, the susceptibility of the industry to future disruption.[67] The report concluded that 63 percent of the companies analyzed were experiencing disruption, and 44 percent were highly susceptible to future disruption.

Accenture focused on large companies with enterprise values of over $100 million, and most of them over $1 billion. Many smaller companies are likely to be much more niched and serving local markets, which reduces their susceptibility to dramatic short-term disruption. Small companies are nimbler and can change direction more easily when they detect a coming disruption to their industry segment. Low susceptibility to disruption is a major component of buyability, so in your business it is important you're aware of the trends and to stay ahead of them.

But the study is relevant to small companies as well, since all businesses go through periods of durability, vulnerability, volatility, and viability, although the cycle time widely varies among them.

In the figure, the lower left quadrant represents durability, industries that enjoy incumbent structural advantages and consistent performance in a sector that attracts relatively few large disruptors. Major industries in this quadrant are consumer goods, chemicals, and industrial equipment. In the durability period, companies need to transform their core business to maintain cost leadership while testing new disruptive ventures.

The next phase in the cycle is vulnerability, where structural weaknesses expose the sector to significant risk, but barriers to entry inhibit disruptor penetration, at least for the time being. Prime examples are banking, utilities, and health, although the latter sector is already entering the volatility phase as COVID-19 leads to the mass postponement of health procedures and the expansion of telemedicine, which receives lower insurance reimbursement rates. In the vulnerability period, incumbents enjoy high barriers to entry, so this is when they need to scale new opportunities.

Companies that face high potential for disruption are in the upper-right volatility quadrant. Here, past sources of strength have become weaknesses, and large disruptors start to unlock fresh sources of value. Infrastructure and transportation, energy, and the postal services sectors are in volatile periods. In the volatility stage, the goal is to retain only the sustainable parts of the core business while investing resources into growing new businesses.

Companies emerging from volatility into viability are embryonic or reborn industries. With high rates of innovation, sources of competitive advantage are short-lived. This is a fast-moving field, including the software and platform, high-tech, and media and entertainment sectors. Companies in the viability stage need to focus on growing their core business by launching new products or pushing existing products into new markets.

Figure 8.3 Accenture's Disruptability Index

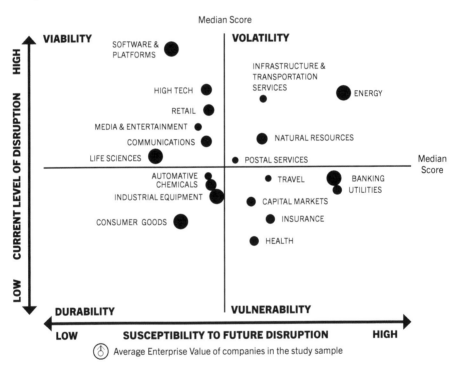

The left-hand quadrants, viability and durability, are the stages it is better for your business to be in to become and remain buyable. Be aware of vulnerable and volatile industries and pivot away or march through them using strategic shifts and innovation.

PULL OUT THE STOPS

This section includes simple strategies that can become game changers for your business. These are perhaps no-brainer concepts, but most business-es don't focus on them because they require discipline and perseverance to execute.

Build a New-Business Engine

No matter how good a business is in servicing and keeping customers, it also has to generate new business consistently. A former client of mine, Landon, the owner of a public relations firm, built a thriving business by serving a handful of accounts really well and helping them grow. The busi-ness was highly profitable, and two of Landon's customers grew from a standing start to more than $100 million in sales revenue.

Landon provided excellent customer service, built a positive culture, assembled a stable team, and his business generated a high double-digit profit margin for many years. Ironically, the only weakness was its lack of a consistent marketing and sales engine inside the business. Landon tried to hire business developers, and they cost a lot of money, but never seemed to work out. He tried outsourcing new-business generation without suc-cess, and then tried to run the sales function himself, but he did not enjoy doing it and his efforts bore little fruit.

He even tried to grow through acquisition, but none of the targets seemed to be a suitable fit.

After several years of single-digit sales and profit growth, one of Landon's two large clients went into Chapter 11. Landon soon realized that without one of his two whales, his business no longer had critical mass, so he shrank the firm down to a personal practice. Had he persisted in developing an internal sales engine and diversified his clientele while the going was good, his business would have survived. Instead, Landon took the easy path and grew by servicing his legacy clients. Over time his business became irreversibly and mortally dependent on them.

Another client, Frank, the owner of a commercial insulation contractor, faced a similar challenge. In its early days Frank's business grew from his personal network, but as it got bigger, this form of growth was no longer sufficient. He tried to groom salespeople in-house with limited success and then outsourced business development to a service called Contractor Connections.

Contractor Connections didn't just attract price-sensitive clients but also took a hefty commission off the top, and Frank's firm had to accept small and low-profit jobs, too, to be considered for more lucrative projects. Relationships with intermediated clients were a lot less personal, which led to more miscommunications and slower payment of bills. The net effect was that Frank's firm racked up a pile of unpaid receivables and its gross margins nosedived. He ended up dismissing Contractor Connections, scaling back the company, and seeking homegrown sales instead.

Finding a star salesperson is not enough. One is the worst number in business. If you have a single person who can sell, your business will be at that person's mercy and eventually she will walk away with your customers, demand to be overcompensated, or burn herself out. Your business will suffer. You need *at least* two salespeople and a marketing function generating leads for them.

Having a sales and marketing engine is a critical ingredient in the recipe for making your business buyable. Don't neglect applying time and attention to building out that function and hiring people to operate it for you.

Maintain a Scalable Cash Flow Profile

I spoke earlier about cash-gobbling businesses. Whenever a small business is in a commoditized sector or is buying from or selling to bigger and more powerful partners, it runs a high risk that its customers and/or vendors will force it to pay early, receive payments late, or hold massive inventories.

The growth of a business that has to finance receivables and inventories is severely limited. Worse still, any money plowed back into receivables and inventories becomes "dead capital." Unless the purchasing and selling structure of the business improves dramatically, which is unlikely, those amounts in a commodity business or a business that deals with powerful partners are tied up in the business forever.

Businesses with the best cash flow profiles are those that pay late and get paid early. Grocery chains, especially ones with a large range of own-brand products, are like that. They sell everything for cash, turn over their in-store inventories in a matter of days, and pay their suppliers 30 to 90 days after delivery. These companies benefit by using their suppliers' cash for 30 to 90 days. Marks & Spencer in the UK was the first grocery store to recycle its cash into a slate of financial products, such as personal loans and investment products, and it launched M&S Bank, which has grown into a top-15 bank in the UK.

A friend of mine, Ottó, built a market-leading contract research organization, called Goodwill Research, from scratch, without capital, by having its international pharma company clients pay him up front on drug-testing contracts. The more contracts Goodwill landed, the more cash it could recycle into hiring and signing up doctors and hospitals to perform research. He scaled fast and eventually sold the business to an Italian public consolidator.

Charging customers a deposit up front is becoming much more common than in the past, and many companies charge customer credit cards upon delivery, which enables them to avoid chasing receivables. Fulfillment businesses can take care of deliveries for you, eliminating the need for your business to hold inventories.

Keep in mind that removing the working capital needs from your balance sheet is a growth superpower.

Nurture a Talent-Attracting Culture

The war over talent is the new frontier in the knowledge economy. Attracting and hiring people have become focus areas for companies, and often the process is trickier than developing new business. Millennials are much choosier about employment than earlier generations, and they want to work for companies with a worthwhile purpose to which they can meaningfully contribute.

Having a talent-attracting culture can be a major asset for a business. One of my clients, Heinan Landa, built Optimal Networks, an MSP serving law firms and associations, into such a company. Heinan and his partner, David Campbell, imprinted their generous and fun-loving personalities onto their firm. They work and play hard and make sure that the people at the company feel they are part of a community that cares about its members. They regularly order food, throw creative events, and sponsor company outings. They award their seasoned employees custom-tailored blue Optimal jackets that are worn as badges of honor.

As mentioned earlier, the fire and flood remediation business, RVA Restoration, not only won the RVA 25 award as the fastest-growing business in Central Virginia but also was chosen as a Top Workplace in the small business category. RVA's owner, Jeremy Ford, cares deeply for his employees and makes sure they are coached, regularly recognized for successes, and catered to. The company lives its core values and is a fun place to work, so it doesn't have a problem finding excellent people—they simply arrive through word-of-mouth recommendations by coworkers and customers.

RVA Restoration's executives also have an ownership mentality. I met with them the day after they won the RVA 25. The plaque was proudly displayed in the conference room. The prize elated Jeremy's team, and executives were speaking over each other about how "their company" was the coolest and how they all loved working on making it great. A couple years earlier, when the company had gone through a rough patch and was not profitable, the same leadership team was adamant that they should consider no bonuses until RVA Restoration was solidly in the black with cash in the bank. Remarkably, they cared for the business as their own, even though none of the six-person leadership team, except for Jeremy, owned stock in the company.

Being attractive to talent is not just about hiring practices. Having employees who live your core values helps you draw in people who want to grow your business and serve your customers as well as you do. Having a strong culture is a major competitive advantage that can't be copied by competitors.

FINE-TUNE THE MACHINE

The impact of the following tactics is perhaps less dramatic, but if you master one or several of them, over time they will ensure that your business delivers best-in-class performance.

Figure Out Your Secret Sauce

Does your business possess a set of durable operating practices that stay stable over time and provide you with a competitive advantage? What is your secret sauce?

Jim Collins articulates the concept of "secret sauce" in *Great by Choice*, calling it the SMaC Recipe.[68] SMaC stands for specific, methodical, and consistent. Collins uses Southwest Airlines as an example. This airline caught up with Delta and United even though it started operating 45 years later than they did. Southwest grew into a contender by consistently following its 10 operating principles:

1. Fly under-two-hour segments
2. 737s only
3. 10-minute turns
4. No air freight or mail
5. No food service

6. No interlining
7. No seat selection
8. Low fares and high frequency
9. Fun family and service culture
10. Bring planes and crews home each night

Connectwise IT, an MSP in Tampa, Florida, presents another successful example of applying the SMaC Recipe.[69] Its operating principles are as follows:

1. Clients within 50 miles
2. Engineers 80 percent billable
3. Hire only fast and smart people
4. Make staff happy. Low turnover
5. Each client issue has an owner
6. 20 percent margin on hardware
7. Recurring revenue from every client
8. Each customer uses at least two offerings
9. Avoid doctors and lawyers
10. No clients with IT departments

Can you articulate your own secret sauce? What do you do for your most profitable and raving-fan clients? What makes sense for you and what works for them? What is your SMaC Recipe?

Establish a Consistent Growth Pattern

In the iconic book *Great by Choice*, Jim Collins talks about the "20-mile march" concept that all dominant businesses have mastered.[70] Collins bases his idea on the story of Robert Falcon Scott and Roald Amundsen, Scottish and Norwegian explorers, respectively, who raced to be the first to reach the Antarctic in 1911. Scott's team took an opportunistic approach and moved with the weather: 70 miles in fair weather and nothing on stormy days. Amundsen's explorers stuck to a 20-miles-a-day quota, no matter the elements. Scott's team lost morale, injured themselves, ran out of food, and died on the way home after finding they were not the first to arrive. Amundsen's team reached the South Pole first and returned home unscathed, with food to spare.

Great companies figure out their 20-mile march, which is the rate of growth they can consistently manage without burning themselves out or running out of money. They then strive to hit their 20-mile march growth goals consistently, year after year. Building a sustainable cadence allows them to rebuild processes, get into a hiring rhythm, innovate consistently, and ensure they either remain cash-positive or build investors' confidence with their consistency and predictability so that investors are happy to fund their growth.

With a consistent growth strategy, your company can turn growth into business as usual rather than the subject of extraordinary efforts that in the long term are not sustainable. Consistency allows better planning and makes it easier to systemize processes and have others execute them for you. Heroic acts can create successful campaigns, but these come at the cost of a later slowdown and loss of key employees who burn out along the way.

One obvious growth bottleneck in small companies is the quality of management. The company can only grow if its top people are expanding their capabilities of managing that growth. They have to keep delegating and elevating themselves. At a 15–25 percent annual growth rate, most of your leadership team may still have a chance to keep pace with the growth of your business. At faster rates of growth, you will likely have to bring higher-caliber people into leadership because probably not all of your team will be able to keep pace. If your business runs on EOS, this will become apparent when some team members stop elevating themselves, start missing their measurables, fail to complete quarterly Rocks, or feel too overwhelmed to engage in solving company-level issues at Level 10 Meetings™.

Outgrowing some of your leadership team members is common and may not be a terrible thing as long as you're ready to make the changes when the time comes.

Shoot for Top Quartile Margins

High-profit-margin companies are very attractive to investors for many reasons. High margins often reflect a powerful brand, a highly effective business model, or a powerful engine of innovation. High profit margins frequently signal differentiation and customer-perceived value creation. Mature companies that have a strong core offering and fixed expenses achieve high margins when scaled, so high profits may also be a sign of scalability.

High-profit-margin companies maintain a strong cushion that enables them to decrease prices and drive out competitors. They also likely nurture competitive advantages that allow them to sustain a leaner cost structure.

How do you improve your profit margins?

Simply put: by increasing revenues and reducing expenses. You can grow revenues by being more aggressive in marketing and sales, differentiating your offerings, and expanding into new geographies and fresh markets for your product. You may also develop new products and services.

Cutting expenses starts with reviewing your cost of goods sold (COGS) or cost of sales (COS), that is, buy cheaper and control labor costs. Apple controls its expenses by building robust supply chains in Asia that include reliable partners and multiple options.[71] Volkswagen reduced its direct manufacturing expenses by developing its "platform strategy": modular cars, where most parts can be used in multiple models. This strategy requires fewer components to be manufactured and decreases the costs of sourcing, training, machining, and storage.[72]

You can also reduce direct costs by moving production to countries with cheaper labor forces, lower infrastructure costs, and state subsidies for companies that bring in foreign direct investment.

Growing sales also helps reduce direct costs by harvesting economies of scale in both production and purchasing.

Expenses other than COGS and COS are called indirect, administrative, or overhead expenses. These costs are not directly linked to the volume of production and include management salaries, head office rent, brand marketing, training, and supporting services fees. Your company can cut overhead, for example, by finding lower-rent office space and streamlining organizational structure by eliminating layers or by outsourcing services to specialist providers or entrepreneurial businesses where the cost of employment is lower.

Researching the best-in-class profit margin in your industry can be a painful but eye-opening experience. If you're not in the top quintile, then it is worth digging deeper into improving your margins to take advantage of the low-hanging fruit that improve profitability.

If you would like to benchmark yourself against your top industry peers, visit: BusinessBenchmarker.com.

Learn from Customer Feedback

Do you have a process for collecting regular customer feedback? Do you know what your customers like and don't like? Are you responsive to your customers' needs? If you don't know exactly what your customers want, you cannot give them the best experience. Becoming aware of their fears, frustrations, and opportunities helps you tailor your services more precisely to their needs.

You can find out what your clients think of your business through surveys, online posts, online reviews, and social media comments, and you can gather this information using internet monitoring tools. Buyable Businesses keep their finger on their customers' pulse and strive to be in tune with them.

Then, use this information to tweak your services, measure satisfaction, improve customer experience and retention, and respond to and manage negative public reactions. By showing your customers that you value their opinions, you get them more engaged with and emotionally connected to your brand.

Listening to your customers will also help you stay ahead of your competition and you'll even be able to spot disruptors sneaking up on you.

KEY IDEAS

- Think of a business as a collection of value drivers and then engineer as many as possible into your company.
- Study each group of value drivers: Finding a Blue Ocean, Pulling Out the Stops, and Fine-Tuning the Machine, and start implementing them, starting with the options that are easiest to execute.
- Finding a Blue Ocean strategy include pivoting to an expanding market and scrutinizing your technologies and business models so that you can escape disruption by others and potentially drive disruption yourself.
- Pulling Out the Stops strategies are concerned with building an internal new-business engine to ensure sustainable independent growth, ensuring your business model is cash-friendly so that you don't have to finance your customers or vendors or be financed by others, and developing a culture magnet for talent to reduce employee churn and improve customer service.
- In Fine-Tuning the Machine, you articulate and ingrain your secret sauce, find your sustainable growth rhythm, benchmark against your top-tier competitors, and continually listen to and learn from your customers.

TOOL FOR THE CHAPTER

Benchmark yourself against your leading industry peers at BusinessBenchmarker.com.

9

GROOM YOUR BUSINESS

János Gréczi is the quintessential self-made entrepreneur. He started importing apparel and nonalcoholic beverages after the fall of the Iron Curtain, and over time he developed the latter concern into a full-fledged beverage distribution business. Later he invested in production equipment using government grants and loans, and by the mid-2000s he owned a thriving bottling empire. He bottled white-label sodas for several international and large domestic grocery chains. He ran a tight ship and made a 25 percent EBITDA margin in a competitive commodity market.

János had a magnetic personality coupled with street smarts, which allowed him to be an extraordinary salesperson and a tough negotiator at the same time. With his exceptional energy and keen eye for diamond-in-the-rough talent like himself, he made all the decisions and delegated execution to a cadre of young, like-minded hustlers.

János approached us in mid-2011 with the goal of selling his business, Gramex, for $30 million. We valued the company at $22 million, but he said he would not sell it before it fetched his Magic Number. We spent the next 18 months helping him groom the company while he also continued to grow the top line. János is a high school graduate, but he has common sense, discipline, and creativity. He implemented every tip we gave him, and grooming actions contributed an extra four percent to his EBITDA margin in 2012.

We ended up selling János's business to a consortium of two private equity funds for over $32 million.

János sold a commodity business as if it were a differentiated one. And it was, while János was there to make the business superior. As soon as he left, however, Gramex's buyers had to hire three seasoned and expensive executives to replace him, which shaved 10 percent off the EBITDA margin. Gramex was no longer an outstanding performer, but it is a perfect case study for effective grooming.

What does grooming a business mean?

When you are seeking a buyer or investor for your business, you want to make the best possible first impression on that buyer and you want to build and maintain trust throughout the process to maximize the valuation of your company. Grooming requires less time than strategic moves such as restructuring the ownership of the company, which we covered in Chapter 7, Lay the Foundation. You can usually take care of grooming steps 6 to 18 months before a sale or financing transaction.

The following sections cover each of the five groups of grooming tactics, including financials, strategy, assets, miscellaneous fixes, and running the business.

Let's start with supercharging your financial statements.

FIX YOUR FINANCIALS

Three Years of Financials

The financial statements are the first and most important lens buyers use to size up your business. Therefore, it is critical that your numbers are reliable, transparent, and consistent. Reliability means that your income statement, balance sheet, and cash flow statement are accurate and backed up by verifiable data. It is worth investing in an audit with a reputable CPA firm to confirm that your financials are true and fair.

Consistency means that you have prepared multiple years of financials that employ the same approach for recognizing revenues and expenses. Companies that reclassify expenses from one year to the next create unnecessary stress and erode the confidence of buyers, who will suspect there is something to hide. Especially when you change accounting or enterprise resource planning software, make sure you maintain consistency of records.

From your financials, buyers also draw conclusions about the quality of your management team. Having historically prepared budgets and forecasts with corresponding actual results available increases confidence that your team is running the business professionally. This shapes expectations that future projections are likely to be reliable and that investors can take them seriously for valuing the potential of the business.

Recast Your Income Statement

Buyers want to understand the profits your business will make for them into the future. They will study your company's historical results to verify whether they should trust your projections as a basis for their valuation. The cleaner your past and the more intentionally you appear to be running the business, the more confident your investors will be that they need not discount your projections. Typically, you present your company's EBITDA, EBIT, or net profit, showing the floor level of profitability the business would deliver and how buyers can grow from there.

Make sure you remove any expenses unrelated to the business and expenses that were one-offs and that will probably not reoccur in the normal course of business. These include the following:

- Expenses incurred for the benefit of the owner that would not be incurred if an independent management team were running the company, such as personal auto expenses, club memberships, payments made to family members over their contributions to the business, salary paid to the owner over what a future CEO with the required skills would earn
- One-time marketing expenses, such as a rebranding campaign or any major nonrecurring marketing initiative
- The cost of design, development, and investment write-offs
- Fire and theft losses

- Lawsuit payments
- Loss on the sale of assets
- Charitable contributions
- Moving expenses

You can usually add back extraordinary expenses as adjustments, but quality of earnings matter, and buyers will question your add-backs and unusual accounting practices. You are best positioned to build trust when you present clean financials and a clear, self-explanatory income statement.

Cut the Nonessentials

In the last full fiscal year before a transaction and in the year of a transaction, spend only on activities that maintain the business's growth or that give you a quick payback. The profitability of these years is paramount in the valuation of your company, and you will recoup every penny saved four to six times over in a higher purchase price.

The year before the sale is not a time for a brand-building campaign. Such activities rarely translate to higher earnings immediately, and their cost will depress profitability in the short term.

This is also not the time to increase payroll, unless an emergency threatens the loss of key personnel.

Review your R&D expenses. Are they all essential to maintain momentum in the year of the planned sale or the year after that, should the transaction fall through? If not, delay them because they will negatively affect your sale price.

The same goes for major capital investments, such as plants and equipment. GAJ, a tier 1 supplier of fabricated steel components to the heavy equipment industry, made a major investment in new computer numerical control machines before its sale to a Swedish public company. The investments were strategic and would support the long-term growth of the business, but the buyers gave no valuation credit for it. Because the outlay reduced GAJ's cash reserves and thus its enterprise value, it practically was a gift to the buyer. The sellers could have avoided giving up what amounted to 20 percent of the sale proceeds if they stopped acting like owners and started acting like sellers in the run-up to the transaction.

Shrink Inventories and Receivables

As discussed in Chapter 3 in the equity value versus enterprise value section, the seller's sale proceeds are the enterprise value of the business (e.g., five times EBITDA) less the net debt the company owes to third parties. The more cash you have tied up in assets, the less money your business has in the bank or the more debt it owes. Every dollar of reduction you can achieve in inventories or receivables directly increases the cash proceeds to you upon a sale.

In the example in Chapter 3, Seph and Roland's business Exdom was worth $8 million on the basis of a multiple of EBITDA. However, the business also owed $8 million to the banks that financed its receivables and inventories. The cost of financing the company's working capital absorbed all its equity value. Had Exdom been able to outsource its fulfillment and sell for cash, the business would have been worth $8 million to its owners rather than zero.

Those sorts of changes in business process may well have been impossible for Exdom to do. This was because the distribution business existed as a way to create a local source of Chinese-manufactured products for big-box retailers that themselves were able to avoid owning inventories and wanted the benefits of free vendor financing. Roland and Seph were in the wrong business, and they were lucky to get out unscathed. The lesson: Avoid bad—unbuyable—businesses, or get out as fast as you can.

In the run-up to the sale, consider ways to cut and outsource your inventories if you can do it cost-effectively. Try to negotiate cash or credit card payments with customers, or involve third-party lending. Financing customers is not your core business and doing it yourself likely will subtract from, rather than add value to your company. It also creates a distraction and harms your cash flow. Avoid factoring receivables because that's probably expensive and most investors consider it as off-balance-sheet debt anyway.

The less inventory and shorter accounts receivable you carry, the more cash will hit your bank account on closing the sale of your business.

When you have fixed your financials, it is time to make your strategy shine.

SELL YOUR STRATEGY

Position Your CEO and Management Team

If you have implemented a Management Blueprint such as EOS, you have already created a management team that is running the business on your behalf. Ideally, you have elevated yourself to the entrepreneur's position and have a full-time manager who runs the day-to-day affairs for you. EOS calls these two roles the Visionary and the Integrator™, respectively. With both a Visionary and an Integrator in place, you can position the business as one that runs without you.

Before the sale, step back even from the Visionary role into the owner's box. What you want is to sell a plug-and-play, self-managing business, and one that is ideally an entrepreneurial company that can drive itself strategically forward. You want to show your investor that the company doesn't need an outside force to stimulate its growth and evolution—it already has these functions built in.

One way to achieve this is by mentoring your Integrator so that person is ready to sell themselves as a credible visionary leader to investors. Have your number two actively immerse themselves in researching market trends; networking with peer companies; taking part in CEO peer groups, such as Vistage, EO, or YPO; and practicing public speaking on the future of the industry and business strategy.

Gino Wickman took his own advice when he sold EOS Worldwide to the Firefly Group in 2018. He had positioned Mike Paton as his Visionary, which allowed Gino to disengage from the operations of his business from the day he sold it.[73]

Know Your Industry Dynamics

The buyers will expect your leaders to understand where your industry is going and how your business will exploit opportunities. Make sure you're on top of industry trends so you can position your business well and make a compelling case to buyers and investors. If you can identify and credibly show the Next Big Thing for your company, you paint an attractive opportunity for buyers. They will be happy to pay full price for your current business when you give them a blueprint on how they could expand it.

The toy distributor Gulliver is a case in point. One of the principal drivers of the sale was that the owners identified a cross-border expansion opportunity into neighboring Romania. Romania had a fragmented toy wholesale and retail market, and the private equity buyer believed that the company could replicate its business model in that market, which was twice the size of Gulliver's home turf.

Beyond entering a new geography, a company may expand into adjacent products by targeting the same consumers by unearthing unmet needs. The questions to ask are: Who is your consumer? What and where do they want to buy? and What price and how can they pay for it?

Another approach is to ask, What job is the customer trying to get done? This question can reveal whether that job is being done well or not, the customer's frustrations, and any barriers limiting consumption. Ask: What can we innovate to serve the unmet need?[74]

Understand and Communicate Value

When you have a good grasp of where your industry is going and understand your competitors and the marketplace, you will have a more realistic picture of the value of your business.

As an M&A advisor, my experience has been that the better the business, the more realistic the owner is of its valuation. Entrepreneurs who feel they have missed the mark in building an excellent business often mentally compensate for their perceived failure by overvaluing their companies.

In selling a business, like in other areas of life, you won't get a second chance to make a first impression. If you approach the market with an apparently high valuation without a logical rationale to support it, investors will roll their eyes and move on.

To get a high valuation, instead of overvaluing the business, focus on executing the following steps:

1. Groom the business properly.
2. Devise a simple plan for how a buyer can grow revenues and profit.
3. Look for synergistic buyers.
4. Create a competitive and high-momentum auction.

If you follow this process, you can achieve a full valuation for your business that corresponds to the stage of the M&A cycle you're in, which is driven by economic expansion, regulatory changes, and the emergence of new technologies. As a result, M&A transaction volumes in the United States have followed a succession of high and low points for over a century now.[75] If you get the timing of the sale right, too, you just might hit it out of the park.

Document PR Initiatives and Testimonials

Your reputation is a key asset to you and your buyer. Make sure you can show a pristine image in your target market and to the public at large with a record of positively received PR activities. Make sure you collect testimonials. Being able to present a list of happy customers can persuade buyers that you have a positive image and service your clients well.

Build and Maintain Your List

One of the most valuable assets a company can have is a list of clients and prospects that know the business and are predisposed to engage with it and become customers. Your investors will want to see that your business has a following and that you have identified, understand, and are nurturing your target market. The size of your list demonstrates how systemized your sales process is and allows for more reliable projections on turning the members of that list into customers.

If you have implemented the EOS Marketing Strategy, you will have already researched your Target Market prospects, what EOS also calls "The List" (see Chapter 6, What Is Your Marketing Strategy), and likely have been promoting to these people. Then, it's just a case of presenting an up-to-date list together with a pipeline of opportunities to your potential buyers and investors.

Be Up Front About Weaknesses

As discussed earlier, building trust with your buyers is paramount because your relationship influences their perception of the quality of your business.

You may have already performed a SWOT analysis as part of your EOS journey. Talking about weaknesses and threats with your buyer builds your credibility because it demonstrates that you're not trying to paint them a rosy and unrealistic picture. By discussing potential negatives, you can show how these could be averted or managed without significant damage to the business.

A proactive approach to negatives allows you to shape the buyer's perception and manage the timing of the release of information on these risks, divulging them when they can do the least damage to your valuation prospects. Buyers are highly likely to discover these issues themselves, anyway, during their due diligence, in which case, if you have not addressed them yet, they may think you're trying to hide things from them. Worse, they might assume that your management was unaware of, and therefore unprepared to mitigate, the risks facing your business.

Every business has competitors, direct and indirect. Being up front and on top of what they are doing is similarly a credibility enhancer and confidence builder with your buyers. Be clear on your positioning vis-à-vis your peers and rivals and how you are planning to enhance your competitive posture. What is your strategy to minimize the threats of competitors and disruptions?

Find Growth with the Resources of Buyers

To maximize your selling price, look for a strategic buyer that could reap cost or revenue synergies, or both, by combining its business with yours. In the event of an interesting match, you should aim to capture a share of the value the synergies create for the buyer. The buyer will be open to giving up some of its synergies if the acquisition is attractive and when you force it to compete with other bidders.

As part of the preparation for a sale, it is important you research the types of synergies that your buyers could realize, such as these:

- **Cost synergies:** When the two companies combine their back offices, which allows them to reduce headcount, or when they can negotiate better terms with their common vendors.
- **Revenue synergies:** Yours and the buyer's businesses can cross-sell each other's products or services. When Facebook bought the 15-month-old and 13-employee-strong Instagram for a billion dollars, it gained access to a new product that it could monetize to Facebook's customers.[76]
- **Talent synergy:** Your acquirer may buy your business to acquire your entrepreneurial or managerial talent. The classic example is Apple's acquisition of NeXT Software, with Steve Jobs returning as CEO.
- **Technology synergy:** Apple's acquisition of NeXT also allowed it to launch the iMac with a new operating system. The Apple–NeXT and the Facebook–Instagram combinations created powerful technology synergies.

- **Financial synergy**: If a public company that is trading at a price-earnings (P/E) multiple of 12 buys your company at a P/E multiple of six, it realizes an instant financial synergy. As part of the acquirer's business, the market could value the earnings of your business at 12 times, also, thereby boosting the share price of the buyer.

Now that your financials and strategy are in great shape, let's take care of your real estate, intellectual properties, and other assets.

POLISH YOUR ASSETS

Outsource Valuable Real Estate

Banks love it when your business owns real estate. Real estate feels much more real to them than your future cash flows and allows them to lend against it to your company. However, investors feel totally different about *your* real estate.

The return expectation from real estate is much lower than what your company should be generating. Most private businesses attract profit (EBITDA) multiples of between four and eight, while a real estate asset could change hands for up to 10–20 times its net income. Thus, any real estate sold as part of a business sells below its market value. You do much better spinning off properties, selling them to a real estate investor, or keeping ownership and leasing them back to your business on market terms.

Most investors are not interested in owning real estate anyway, because it makes it harder for them to generate a competitive return on their investment. Both strategic buyers and private equity funds focus on investing in either business assets, which they can grow for a higher return, or real estate assets, which will generate a lower but predictable return, requiring less attention. They rarely want both.

The exception is when your real estate can't be profitably utilized out-

179

side of the business. This would be the case with a plant in the middle of the countryside or a piece of highly specialized property that is difficult to convert cost-effectively to new use.

Spin off real estate from your business. Then, let's see whether your business should even be using it.

Optimize the Locations of Your Premises

You need not own your premises, but you have to have them in the right location. Consider moving your business out of the city if real estate or rent is expensive or if you have no room to grow there. Multiple locations are often worth merging to make them more efficient and manageable. Get out of an expensive lease, if you can, to improve your profit and valuation in a new location. Or lengthen your lease well before a transaction to avoid being at the mercy of your landlord when you are selling your business and they know you're under time pressure.

I worked on the sale of a business that distributed wheelchairs, orthopedic shoes, and other medical consumables. Its warehouse was full, and the buyer, which wanted to use the business's storage facilities also to distribute its own auxiliary products, refused to close the deal until the seller moved into an expanded location. Because of time pressures, reasonably priced appropriate real estate was scarce, which delayed the deal, almost causing it to fall through, but eventually the buyer relented.

Make sure you optimize your location well in advance of a transaction, when you have time to negotiate a good solution.

Fix Environmental and Safety Issues

Next to location, perceived environmental risk can be another impediment to selling your business or getting investors onboard. If you cannot eliminate this risk, your buyer may require you to guarantee it. This could end up costing you exorbitantly if they want you to fix any issues at your cost, just before your indemnities expire.

During the sale of machine fabricator GAJ, discussed earlier, a loss-making foundry owned by GAJ almost sank the sale. The buyer saw a potential environmental and PR disaster in the making. Therefore, it wanted the sellers to buy out or close the foundry before it would purchase GAJ.

The sellers were private individuals who were ready to retire and had no interest in taking over a subsidiary, let alone a failing business. They loathed the thought of firing the 40 people who worked at the foundry, because this would hurt their legacy in their hometown. Some locals already accused them of "selling out their employees" to an international buyer that was a stranger in their city. Thus, the last thing the sellers needed was to be causing layoffs and the liquidation of the foundry.

Eventually, the foundry's management expressed interest in buying the ailing plant for a nominal price. As it turned out, after the sale, the new owners achieved a complete turnaround. Apparently, the night before the buyout they walked home as employees who could not fix their loss-making business. But the next day they walked back in as owners with no time and money to waste. The business became profitable overnight and stayed in the black for the next two years. Eventually, quality issues and a shrinking market forced them into liquidation.

Make sure you fix environmental issues or be prepared to handle them during the negotiations. The next thing to worry about is the optics of the business. Buyers will walk the plant, and their impressions influence the price and possibly even the buyability of your business.

Refresh and Tidy Up the Business

We promoted a family-owned flexographic printer that developed a diverse slate of large FMCG customers in the food and packaging industry. The business had an innovative product and healthy profit margins and was growing by 20 percent per annum. The business was fairly small, with about $7 million in sales and $1.5 million of EBITDA.

We received an attractive offer from another family-owned company about five times our client's size. This potential buyer was looking for an entry point into the flexographic printing space. It issued a letter of intent and was about to start due diligence using a Big Four CPA firm. The buyer's CEO asked to visit the company to gain a personal impression before the buyer sent in auditors.

Unfortunately, our client was ill prepared for the visit—partially our fault because we had not visited the premises for some time and didn't realize the messy state it was in. The owner had old machines, which had not been cleaned, and pieces of unused materials and equipment laid around, creating risk of injury. Worst of all, the building was in ill repair, with peeling paint. The factory made a poor overall first impression.

In contrast, the buyer kept a pristine facility, and cleanliness was an important part of the values and image of its business. Our client's company didn't impress the buyer, and it turned down the ownership opportunity, in the meantime paying a backhanded compliment to the sales memorandum, which "made the business look great."

Be sure to clean up and even paint the building and your equipment. Make it as pristine and fresh as you can. First impressions can turn out to be the last.

Protect Your Intellectual Property

If you have built a differentiated business, likely you own intellectual property (IP) such as patents and trademarks that represent value. Buyers and investors will want to see that you have documented and fully protected such IP and that it is free of litigation. Any IP you have not registered or documented raises a red flag for the buyer, who will assume that that property is at risk or might even be owned by others. Without secure IP, your business may be worth a lot less and may not even be an interesting target for a prospective investor.

Unfortunately, patent and trademark processes take months, and their ownership can be challenged by third parties or even by an investors' straw men, who may use such weaknesses to renegotiate the acquisition. IP issues can delay and ultimately kill deals when business, market, or economic circumstances shift and the deal stops making sense or being a priority for your counterpart.

IP protection is almost always a formality, but it must be done thoroughly and well in advance.

The last asset to protect—which might be the most important—is your CEO and other key executives.

Key Person Insurance

Insuring your business's key people can be an important move when the buyer will rely on the ongoing contributions of the seller or a handful of hard-to-replace executives. Taking out insurance seems easy to do at the last minute, but I learned the hard way that it isn't.

We represented a middle-aged construction entrepreneur, Mr. Bromfeld, who owned a general contracting company that worked extensively for municipalities in and around Budapest. He was in poor health and had a stressful job dealing with local politicians. He had to entertain them constantly and help them with favors and in other ways.

Mr. Bromfeld's business was growing and profitable, and it had a diverse and loyal customer base, which caught the attention of a French construction group. They liked the business and issued a letter of intent for the acquisition of a 51 percent initial stake followed by a full buyout over the next three years. Mr. Bromfeld, after some negotiations, accepted.

The due diligence went okay, too, and the contract negotiations also progressed well until we hit an unexpected landmine: Mr. Bromfeld was overweight, had high blood pressure, and was unwell. Sensing his unsound condition to be a risk to the business, the buyer required that the company take out key man insurance on the CEO. The policy would then be assigned to the buyer as beneficiary to mitigate the risk that Mr. Bromfeld might become incapacitated during the seller–buyer cohabitation period. In particular, the buyer fretted that the well-connected founder's successor would not be able to maintain Mr. Bromfeld's business relationships with local municipalities. This could potentially diminish the value of the business.

Mr. Bromfeld flatly refused, stating that a key man life insurance policy would put a target on his back, and the buyers might try to get rid of him to recover their investment should the company underperform under their ownership. The buyer eventually backed down from its demand, but the seller's trust was already shattered. Mr. Bromfeld promptly withdrew from the deal and continued to manage the company for six more years before turning it over to a minority owner-manager.

Make sure that the company is insured for the loss of its key executives so that there is time and money for it to recover should one of its key people pass. Imagine if, in the event of your incapacitation or death, your family had to take over running your business or find a buyer without trusted management in place. Such a scenario could potentially wipe out the value of your business and harm your family and personal legacy.

Now that your financials, strategy, and assets are polished, let's groom the remaining areas of your business.

COVER YOUR BASES

Organize Data and Records

Being organized makes a positive impression and reassures a buyer that your business is well run. Ideally, be sure all the numbers on your income statement and balance sheet are supported by detailed accounting records and contracts when relevant. Larger companies invest in a vendor due diligence (VDD) done by a CPA firm before going to market to ensure that the company is clean and organized and that they discover and can fix any issues before buyers show up.

If you don't have the budget for a full-fledged VDD from a big accounting firm that does due diligence for a living, you can ask your CPA or even your M&A advisor to help bring a fresh set of eyes and a VDD checklist to cover all the bases.

Some years ago, as mentioned earlier, MB Partners advised Ottó Skorán, the owner of Goodwill Research, a leading contract research organization, when an Italian public company wanted to buy his business. Goodwill was a fast-growing, highly entrepreneurial business, but not very organized. The bid came out of the blue. Weeks before the customary August shutdown in Italy, when most business activity slows to a standstill, the potential buyer issued a letter of intent and hired a Big Four accounting firm to conduct a financial due diligence. The buyer was eyeing a competing acquisition, and Goodwill was one of only two businesses it would acquire that year.

We had only a week and two weekends to prepare and organize the data room from scratch, including creating much of the documentation and reconciliations that the buyer was expecting to see. If we couldn't provide them in time, Goodwill would lose credibility and the Italians would move on to buy their other target.

We hired a friend who was a Big Four–trained CPA on sabbatical, and she jumped right in to organize the data room, creating all the missing documentation. She, along with Ottó's finance staff, worked around the clock, and we ended up presenting a nearly complete picture of a previously underdocumented entrepreneurial organization. The sale closed right after the August holidays.

Being well prepared to show the buyer around your business is a high-return investment. Don't skimp on a vendor due diligence when you are getting ready for a transaction. Having an advance view and time to correct issues will increase your credibility, buyer interest, and leverage in controlling the sale or financing process. Having a VDD has the additional benefit of making the opportunity to invest in your company cheaper and more accessible to potential suitors. Thus, more buyers will likely consider your opportunity and the increased interest often translates into higher bids.

Beyond accurate information, you want to make sure your key people will stay with your business during and after the transaction.

Make Stay-Put Arrangements

For your buyer to be willing to pay for maximum value, keep your key employees through, and sometimes beyond, the sale of your business. Some of them may feel threatened by a new owner or reluctant to continue if you're no longer their employer. Sometimes they would even want to jump ship before the transaction closes so they can negotiate a new job elsewhere from an employed position, that is, before their fired colleagues flood the job market.

You can often keep these key people by offering them a stay-put bonus payable at the closing of the sale or at multiple future dates if the buyer pays you in installments. You want to make sure that your best people will be there to contribute to the company throughout your earn-out period, and possibly even for the period covered by your representations and warranties, to maximize the sale proceeds.

Solt, who sold electrical contractor Epsillon to a Dutch construction company, stayed for the full four-year warranty period he granted the buyer. He wanted to make sure, from the CEO position, that the buyer would not be tempted to try to recover part of the purchase price through warranty claims.

Make sure that your key employees stay—and you may do so, too—to ensure a full payout.

Ensure Contracts Are Transferable

A type of commercial contract allows customers or vendors to cancel upon an ownership change in your business. These contract clauses are there to protect them from a situation in which your company inadvertently shares trade secrets or creates conflict situations if it were to fall into the hands of a competitor of your customers or vendors.

Buyers can get nervous when they see such clauses in contracts and will want to speak directly with your vendors and customers before the transaction to confirm that they would not cancel those contracts. This conversation is rarely productive because the news of the transaction can desta-bilize vendor and customer relationships and employees might get jittery, too.

It is better to address these issues 12 to 18 months before the planned transaction, when vendors and customers are happy with the relationship, when a contract renewal gives occasion to negotiating a change, or when you can offer something in return for removing that clause from your agreements.

Comply with Regulations and Licenses

Buyers worry that the business they acquire might be out of compliance with laws and regulations. Such a state of affairs can create an unknown financial and legal exposure, not just for the purchased business but also for the deeper-pocketed buyer entity. Acquirers therefore try to protect themselves against the maximum exposure, which is often significant compared to the purchase price. Safeguarding the buyer means less money or more risk for the seller. Such dynamics can create challenges to con-cluding a transaction.

Full and documented compliance can boost the buyer's confidence, especially if it is an institutionalized corporation. You will find it worth-while to hire a specialist attorney to scrutinize the field to ensure that your business fully complies with all regulations and is up-to-date with all re-quired licenses. Make sure you voluntarily clean up the consequences of any past lapses before your buyers spot them and potentially blow them out of proportion.

Resolve Litigations and Rectify Liabilities

Outstanding litigations against your business can make a sale difficult to consummate. Lawsuits cast a cloud over the activities of the business and create an open-ended liability that can reduce the business's value, sometimes significantly. It's best to resolve litigation before going to market, but start early, because rushing legal cases or pursuing an out-of-court settlement strengthens the other side's negotiating position and can cost you.

One effective solution I've seen is when the parties to the sale agree that the seller will take charge of the case. The seller negotiates on behalf of the company in return for indemnifying the business for any losses that may result. Unfortunately, some buyers don't accept that solution, fearing that the seller might agree to a settlement that casts a negative light on the company or because it might drag out the case unduly in hope of an unlikely outcome.

A client I mentioned earlier, the wheelchair company, was litigating for substantial damages and felt confident that it would win its case. The buyer was skeptical and refused to pay for the bounty the seller expected and did not believe in pursuing the case. The case came off as a distraction to the buyer, which focused on integrating the acquired business.

The owner of the wheelchair business decided to sell the assets of the business and keep the legal entity, which continued to pursue the litigation. This solution was a win for the buyer, too, because acquiring assets, instead of the company, saved her the cost of financial due diligence. She also avoided having to negotiate representations and warranties to mitigate the risks of buying a "black box" entity with unknown liabilities.

Devise a Data-Disclosure Strategy

A business courting buyers always risks espionage by competitors that pose as bidders or by legitimate buyers that decide during the transaction to acquire the business on the cheap. They might poach key people, steal sensitive client or pricing information, spy on R&D activities and proprietary processes, or otherwise steal business secrets.

You can only eliminate espionage exposure by pulling your business from the market. But you can minimize the risk with careful planning and preparation, and the disciplined execution of a piecemeal information-sharing strategy.

While exploring a transaction, the parties gradually get to know each other and negotiate. They build trust with each other. You can manage your disclosure risk by drip-feeding sensitive information, timing the drip to mirror the level of comfort that you have gained with your acquirer.

The gradual approach requires your counterpart to build their commitment by investing CEO or senior executive time and attention in the process. CEOs rarely have the time or willingness to put their personal reputation at stake by conducting a pretense of diligence and contract negotiations just to spy on a competitor. They might, however, be willing to spy through lower-level executives because they avoid exposing themselves as part of a dubious maneuver.

During the sale of heavy machinery fabricator GAJ, the owner group of late-middle-age engineers were highly skeptical of the process. They refused to make concessions to the buyer's M&A team, staffed by thirty-something yuppies with flashy MBAs. GAJ's owners did not trust these suits enough to share sensitive information. At the same time, the undisclosed facts were critical for the Swedish acquirer to review before it could proceed with the acquisition.

It wasn't until a gray-haired senior vice president of the buyer, Elias, showed up that negotiations finally got over the hump. He was an engineer himself, had a strong personal presence, understood GAJ's business, used the right analogies, and applied humor to break the tension when necessary. Elias had to pay several visits to build sufficient trust with the sellers in order for them to start sharing secrets and making needed concessions.

Have a viable strategy on how you will share information with the buyer so that you expose sensitive data only in proportion to the commitments the buyer is willing to make.

RUN YOUR BUSINESS

I've left the best for last.

This is the most important grooming strategy of all. If you follow only one suggestion from this chapter, embrace this one. In my fifteen-year career as an M&A advisor, the single biggest killer of business sales I witnessed was when owners relaxed their intensity and allowed the business to falter.

The advice to continue running your business at full tilt is easier stated than done. When you finally decide to sell your business, your vision for it starts to disappear. The future of your company is no longer your future, and your motivation to focus on it dissolves. Many CEOs ponder the next stage of their life, including freedom from the stress of running the business and lifestyle changes their expected financial windfall will facilitate.

Focusing on the often mundane task of running the day-to-day operations is challenging when you no longer fear the threat of failure or embrace the promise of your organization's vision. Especially when there is the distraction of a much more intriguing sale process, which you may feel requires your full attention.

At MB Partners, the sellers we worked best with were those clients who fully entrusted and empowered us to manage their sale process while they continued to shepherd the business forward. They followed our strategic and tactical guidance and let us coordinate communications with investors and buyers on their behalf. We didn't always succeed in selling their business, for various reasons, but when we did, the results were off the charts. These clients disciplined themselves to keep the business growing and stayed profitable during the sale process, which often took longer than a year.

A classic trap is allowing the buyer to undermine your advisor so that the two principals can do the deal "head to head." The trouble with this notion is that acquisitive businesses often use seasoned professionals with dozens of deals under their belts, while sellers are first-timers. It is easy to see how the imbalance of information and experience can work in the former's favor.

Some buyers are professional seducers, great at courting sellers and gaining their trust and confidence, which they then exploit by driving win–lose deals. The more you get involved in the sale of your business, the more distracted you become, and the likelier you will lose focus on managing the business. The buyer may promise to close in 60 days, but inevitably questions keep coming up and transactions drag out. The time invariably works against you, the seller, creating opportunities for the buyer to react to any adverse event by reducing the offer.

Even in a stable environment, six months in to a transaction, your continued distraction will start showing in softening revenue and profit numbers, cueing the buyer to reopen price negotiations. Your growth momentum broken, you either agree to a lesser deal or shelve the transaction for another 18 to 24 months to rebuild your business before returning to the market.

I cannot overemphasize the importance of mental discipline and focus, giving all you've got to the business during the time of the sale. In the middle market, a sale often takes 12 to 18 months or longer to consummate. Be prepared to resist the siren songs you will start hearing as soon as you have hired a banker and visualized the sale of your business. Your long-term vision and the fear of failure that have driven you to succeed in your business will immediately disperse, sapping your motivation. The anticipated windfall your banker has promised will trigger irresistible thoughts of alluring holidays, boats, and houses you might buy, and other businesses you may start. The best coping mechanism is to assume that the sale will fall through and that you must be prepared to return to the market two years from now with a company that has maintained its growth momentum.

KEY IDEAS

- Don't leave money on the table by neglecting simple best practices that position your business for a seamless and full-value transaction. Give yourself 12 to 18 months before a potential transaction to execute the grooming process.
- Start with whipping your financials into shape. Cut nonessential expenses and add back personal ones. Be sure to minimize your working capital needs.
- Position the CEO and leadership team as the people running the

business. Make sure they understand the industry dynamics and can articulate the opportunities that would grow the business. Be up front with buyers about problems and potential synergies so you can negotiate a higher price.

- Outsource your valuable real estate and make sure your business is in the right place at the right price well in advance of a deal. Make sure environmental issues are handled, IP is registered, and your plant and office shine before the buyer calls on you.
- Be well organized for the due diligence. Ensure contracts are transferable, licenses are up-to-date, and their contingent liabilities are minimal. Keep the support of key people with retention bonuses.
- Decide how you will share information with buyers to minimize abuses by competitors.
- Make sure you work with M&A professionals you trust, and let them handle the sale while you focus on running your business through a transaction as if it was business as usual.

PART FOUR:
CONSTRUCT YOUR IDEAL LIFE

If you have followed this guide so far, you now have a self-managing, fast-growing, and high-profit business, one that has been groomed for a harvesting transaction. It is truly a Buyable Business and will have no problem attracting interested buyers and investors. You might have already been approached by several who have noticed your evolution.

Now that your Buyable Business gives you options, the only thing left to do is decide what you want to do. First, you decide on how you will harvest your business. In this part, I walk you through what a transaction looks like so you know what to expect. Your decision about which M&A advisor or investment banker to pair with is critical for a seamless transaction that yields an optimal outcome. We will review your options to help you decide what, if any, role you want to play in the future of the company. Finally, before pulling the trigger, I invite you again to think hard about your post-transaction life and what is worth retiring for. A compelling Next Chapter makes building a Buyable Business well worth all the effort.

(10) HOW TO CASH IN

This chapter reviews the ways and the tools you can use to harvest your Buyable Business to raise the funds required for your Next Chapter.

In it I also discuss the variables of business sale and capital transactions. Your preferred way to monetize your company depends on your desire to maximize your payout tempered by your aversion to the risk of losing part of the purchase price to potential claims under the representations and warranties you agreed to and by your relationship with the people who remain in the business.

Finally, I'll point out other considerations that influence the type of transaction you will choose to undertake, including what happens if you stay with the business after the deal. Is partnering with private equity desirable for you? We'll cover the pros and cons of employee share ownership programs and initial public offerings.

HARVESTING EQUITY

You Don't Have to Sell Your Business

To harvest your Buyable Business, you don't always have to sell it. Sometimes, you don't even have to give up minority ownership in your business.

In 2007, the founder of a successful civil construction business, József Szabadics, approached us. As I touched upon in Chapter 2, József had built his business from scratch to more than $30 million in sales and $6 million in EBITDA. His two sons were helping him run the business, and the younger one, Zoltán, was preparing to take over as CEO. József had three objectives: He wanted to retire, he wanted to transition the business to his sons, and he wanted to take enough chips off the table so that his family, including his children, would be set for life.

Szabadics was a dominant company with high market share in regional municipal water and sewage plant construction projects. Further, the business had the potential to tap a coming wall of money that Hungary would receive from the first European Union budget cycle of 2007–2013.

At first, we attempted a majority sale and attracted half a dozen strategic and private equity investors to look at the business. However, none of the bidders proceeded to issue an LOI. They were afraid of not being able to sustain higher-than-usual profit margins and were concerned about maintaining the local business relationships the Szabadics family had cultivated over decades of building personal connections.

Next, we tried to arrange a recapitalization with a private equity investor. The Szabadics family would have sold a minority stake to generate the liquidity József wanted to ensure the financial independence of his family. The deal faltered when both private equity funds wanted to limit the payout to 20 percent of the value of the business.

Szabadics was a fantastic business, and I felt frustrated that we couldn't help József with the transaction. As a last resort, we tried a deal structure that we had done for a heating equipment manufacturer two years earlier: a recapitalization without a financial sponsor.

We called it a "self-buyout" because it worked like a bank-funded management buyout with an important exception: Neither the seller nor the buyers wanted to offer a personal guarantee. It would have defeated the purpose of de-risking the Szabadics family, and József could not have retired with the stress that he might have to jump back in to save the business.

The transaction involved some financial engineering with two holding companies and mergers. (See Figure 10.1.) But the net effect was that József could fully exit, while his two sons, Zoltán and Attila, acquired 90 percent of the shares, with the remaining stake going to a newly hired president.

Figure 10.1 How a "Self-Buyout" Works

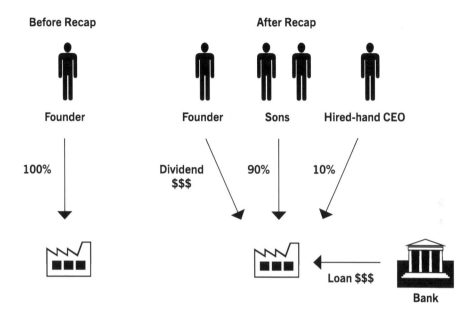

It took some legwork to find a bank that was comfortable taking a full risk on the business without the guarantee. But one was willing to do it. Szabadics borrowed two and a half times its shareholders' equity to pay out 60 percent of the enterprise value as dividend to József. The Szabadics family had their cake and ate it too.

The bank also did well. Five years and a recession later, it got its loan back in full with interest.

A sponsorless buyout of your business is an unusual transaction. Let's look at other more frequently applied investment structures that you may choose to harvest your Buyable Business.

Tools to Harvest Equity

You have several tools at your disposal to access the equity in your business, the most common ones being: strategic buyout, private equity buyout, recapitalization with private equity, recapitalization with bank debt, management buyout, private placement, and employee stock ownership plan. You can choose the one that fits your financial and lifestyle objectives while also matching your personal risk tolerance. (See Figure 10.2.)

Figure 10.2 Cash Out versus Price/Risk Retained

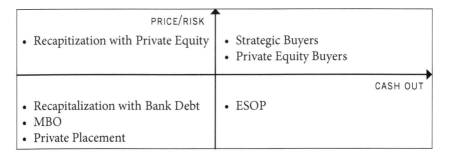

The tool that you should use depends on whether you want to

- Maximize your purchase price or minimize your risk
- Maximize your payout on closing a transaction or maximize your total sale proceeds
- Optimize your financial outcome or optimize your personal relationships
- Stay involved in the business or leave in the short to midterm
- Grow as fast as possible or grow slower while maintaining control
- Maximize tax breaks or minimize red tape

Let's dive into each of these scenarios to see how these tradeoffs arise.

MAXIMIZING DOLLARS

Maximizing Purchase Price versus Minimizing Risk

If your priority is to maximize your purchase price, consider choosing an institutional buyer, such as a strategic acquirer or private equity fund. If you own a Buyable Business that is making at least $2 million in EBITDA and double-digit net margin with potential to grow, you can expect multiple strategic and private equity buyers to compete for the privilege of investing in your company. Because of fierce competition and an abundance of public and private capital seeking quality opportunities, they will pay top dollar for the right opportunity.

On the flip side, be careful when dealing with institutional investors. You will need the help of top-notch advisors to negotiate for you, and you will still end up carrying much of the risk of your business after the transaction. These buyers will demand that you stand behind every risk that originated with your business before the date of closing. They will expect you to represent and warrant every asset on your balance sheet and indemnify the buyer for any litigation, penalty, employee dispute, patent infringement, and so forth that may emerge because of anything your business did, didn't do, or should have done in the past. Whether you know about it or not.

Solt ended up having to provide indemnities for four years after he sold his electrical contracting business, Epsillon, to Dutch strategic buyer Janzzen. He was unhappy with having to provide such extensive warranties and stayed put as CEO until his commitments expired. He made sure they would log no unreasonable claims in his absence and that he would be present to defend the company of any justifiable claims to minimize his losses.

If your priority is to have a clean transaction with no recourse from the buyer, then you should try selling in "easier" ways:

- Sell your business to your own management team in a **management buyout**. They have been running the business alongside you and should know all the hidden risks and not need your warranties to mitigate them.

- **Recapitalize the business** using nonrecourse bank funding from a bank that knows and trusts your business or one that is desperate to have your company become its client. Szabadics got funding from one such outside bank, because incumbents are often too complacent to stretch.
- Raise money through a **private placement** with investors who trust you and see the potential in your business. Private placement investors don't invest for a living and will probably be more hands-off than strategic or private equity buyers are.
- Sell your business to an **ESOP**.

You can be in full control of the transaction and avoid providing any representations or warranties. But the company will probably take years to pay you in full. A management consulting firm in Virginia was sold to an ESOP led by an incoming CEO. The seller left the management team but had to return as an advisor to save the business. Unfortunately for him, he no longer held management rights, which made his job of rescuing the business doubly hard.

Maximizing Payout on Closing versus Maximizing Total Sale Proceeds

To maximize payout on closing, build a self-managed, high-potential, and clean business that multiple institutional buyers compete for. Most times, they will buy 100 percent of the stock for cash, subject to receiving indemnities from you that protect them for undisclosed losses or claims against the business. This is attractive when you want to exit immediately, are sick of running the business, or expect an economic downturn that would reduce the value of your company.

Alternatively, you may want to maximize the sales proceeds you can capture over a longer time period, being fearful of keeping all your assets tied up in the business. By cashing in some chips, you could remove your personal and family financial concerns. With these risks off your shoulders, you could take a chance on growing the business aggressively, reaching for your full potential as an entrepreneur. If so, pick a private equity partner that will buy some of your stock and inject growth capital into the business in cash or through bank borrowing.

One of my clients, New Jersey–based spend and revenue management company Corcentric, recently received a minority equity investment to speed up its global expansion through further acquisitions. This transaction allows the founders of the company to expand more rapidly without ceding control.[77] President Matt Clark told me that growing the business faster with a partner enabled the founders to capture more value than if they had continued to fund growth from their own resources.

Optimizing Financial Outcome versus Optimizing Personal Relationships

Earlier-mentioned Computa was a $40-million-in-sales-revenue data-mining business in Virginia Beach, owned by its CEO, Drew, and CFO, Jason, who bought the business from its founder 10 years earlier. Drew and Jason wanted to sell the business and hired me to find a buyer.

There was tremendous interest in the company, but most investors pulled back when they realized that Computa had a customer concentration issue. One bidder that stayed could dilute the concentration by absorbing the business into its competing activities, which served different customers. That bidder was a strategic investor out of New York and it wanted to move production from Virginia to its own plant. This would have led to significant layoffs immediately, and Computa would have disappeared from Virginia as soon as the buyer moved the plant to New York and replaced key employees.

Drew and Jason decided that they would not abandon their people and their legacy and so rejected the offer. Soon after, they withdrew their business from the market altogether and sold it to an ESOP instead. This solution promised them a smaller payout, spread over several years, but the business they built continued to prosper as an independent company, together with their employees and their families.

Contrast this with Tibor, who sold Tellogen, a logistics management software developer to a top 10 European IT company. Tibor, a highly autonomous seller, was not comfortable with the politics of a complex international organization, so he negotiated an early exit and resigned his CEO position. Tibor made a clean break and started a new business with his minority partner rather than adapt to a corporate environment.

OTHER CONSIDERATIONS

Staying Involved versus Leaving Soon

Many of us became entrepreneurs because we think building a business can be fun. It is a noble adventure that you can do ethically while being a role model and helping other people. Being in charge of a growing and prosperous enterprise is exhilarating and purposeful. When you have reached a point where you have delegated all that you are not good at and don't like to do, why would you trade your job for a low-impact retirement?

Years ago, I advised Mr. Kwan, a Korean businessman in his mid-seventies, who ran a plastic injection molding company that manufactured TV monitors for Samsung in a remote Hungarian village outside Budapest. I helped Mr. Kwan with several financing and equity transactions over the years, and he gradually opened up and shared stories about his past ventures and motivations.

I learned that he was a US citizen and his wife and friends lived in an affluent New Jersey neighborhood. I was astonished to learn that he would choose to live in the Hungarian countryside managing 300 employees instead of playing golf in a plush suburb of New Jersey. Apparently, his friends envied him for holding an important position and tackling meaningful business challenges while being responsible for hundreds of families. Mr. Kwan felt powerful, had fun daily, and was on a mission. Stress was a tolerable price.

If you want to stay involved for the long haul, then your solution may well be to de-risk your business and put money away to create peace of mind for yourself and your family. This then liberates you to give your all to your business going forward. With money in the bank, you can pull out all the stops and become all you can be.

However, your chief purpose may lie outside of the business, as did Csaba's of Gulliver, whose love was ice hockey. He made sure he could be completely out of the business within months after closing. With a full cash payment in the bank.

Growing Fast with Professionals versus Growing Slower with "Friendlies"

If you are confident that you can handle the high expectations of a venture capital or private equity investor, then you can swing for the fences.

When your business has a strong batting average and a compelling vision, these institutional investors will throw as much money at you as you need to scale your business. You might even hit a home run, become wealthy, and keep control of the business at the same time.

On the flip side, your investors will quickly replace you if you don't perform to expectations. Should the business lose value, they will have no qualms about diluting your equity stake by raising a fresh round of capital.

If you are more conservative and less hungry for the big leagues, try working with softer partners. Recapitalize the business with the help of a bank, like Szabadics did, or raise money through a private placement from high-net-worth individuals.

Banks want to make sure you service your debt and will only push you out in critical circumstances when your business's survival is at stake. Private placement investors will be hands-off as well, as long as there is hope you will repay them and even beyond. However, if your business doesn't make money, you will have to put up with nervous phone calls and harassing letters from wealth advisors or attorneys.

A home health services entrepreneur from Virginia Beach who was backed by a private placement told me how painful it was to deal with disappointed local private investors. He eventually found a venture fund to buy them out so he could deal with a competent, albeit more professionally demanding, equity partner.

Maximizing Tax Breaks versus Minimizing Red Tape

For the business owner who is skeptical of buyers, risk averse, willing to stick around, and adamant about leaving a legacy for employees, an ESOP may be the right solution.

An ESOP allows you to manufacture an acquirer from thin air, one who will buy your business financed by bank loans and tax breaks. The downside of an ESOP is that unless your business is highly bankable, you may have to stick around for a while to get fully paid off.

The carrot is Uncle Sam's generous tax breaks for selling to an ESOP trust, including deferral and possible exemption from capital gains taxes on the shares the ESOP buys from you. Your former company can then pay "reasonable dividends" tax-free to its new owner, the ESOP trust, which will then pay off the bank loan that funded the buyout.[78] See Figure 10.3 for a diagram of how an ESOP works.

Figure 10.3 Basic Structure of an ESOP

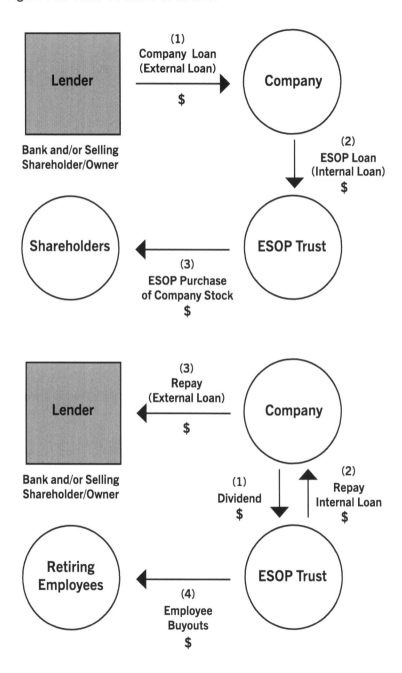

Many entrepreneurs prefer not to sell to an ESOP because of the administrative burdens and expenses involved. These include the costs of third-party administration, valuation, trustee and legal services, and the buyback of vested shares when employees retire or leave. The purchase price the ESOP can pay is capped at the fair value of the shares, whereas the seller might receive a higher price from a synergistic buyer.

Are Public Markets an Option?

Initial public offerings (IPOs) are typically for maturing companies that have surpassed $100 million in revenue, are growing by at least 30 percent a year, and have in place a management team that envisions building a billion-dollar company in the foreseeable future. To satisfy these criteria, the company has to be a significant player in a large, addressable market, with the potential to shake off competition and expand its offerings. The business also has to have an early and predictable path to positive cash flow and profitable growth.

Even if your business is ticking all the boxes, doing an IPO is time consuming and expensive. According to Big Four accounting firm PricewaterhouseCoopers (PwC), the average IPO takes 12 to 18 months to plan and six to nine months to execute. It also costs more than $4 million in fees and at least 4 percent of the proceeds of the offering.[79]

The road to an IPO in most cases leads through earlier venture or private equity investment rounds. These investors help coach and drive management to shape the business into an IPO-ready product. Better to start with a private sale or capital raise.

KEY IDEAS

- You don't have to give up control to monetize your company. The beauty of having a Buyable Business is that you have options.
- Choose the transaction type that best matches your needs, risk profile,

and desired lifestyle. Answer the following questions to decide:

- Do you want to maximize your sale price or minimize your headaches?
- Are your personal legacy and employees important, or do you just want to take the cash and get on with your life?
- Do you want to take chips off the table now and have another bite of the apple later?
- If so, how aggressively do you want to grow the business?
- In exceptional circumstances you might arrange a sponsorless recapitalization, which allows you to harvest your nest egg from the company you own and continue as the major shareholder.

11

EXECUTE A TRANSACTION

It was chilly Monday morning, February 3, 2014. My partner Róbert and I arrived at eight at the Budapest offices of White & Case on Andrássy Boulevard. The law firm was already swarming with attorneys, many of them having spent the night poring over documents, crossing t's and dotting i's. Today the largest business sale in MB Partners' history would take place, and it was the last day Róbert and I would be in the company's employ.

We were cautiously optimistic but keeping our cool because days like this could end with us feeling euphoric, relieved, or numb. We had been working for nearly two years to put this deal together. We believed in the deal so much that we had kept it outside of the sale of MB Partners the previous summer.

A lot was on the line for both of us. Róbert had spent 80 percent of his time on this transaction, and if we failed to close, he would kick himself for not taking that lucrative job with KPMG. For me, closing the sale would mean paying off vendors, a mortgage, buying out my former partners, and buying a home in Virginia, where my family and I had moved to 18 months earlier.

The day had started auspiciously, but our clients János and Tímea Gréczi arrived half an hour late to the meeting. (I later learned the two owners of Gramex had been sitting in their car debating whether to go through with the sale.) Without greeting the advisors, János pulled me into a compact meeting room to share his and Tímea's concerns. Was this deal really a good idea? he asked. Wouldn't he be better off keeping the business, having just turned 40? What would he be doing without running and growing Gramex? Being an entrepreneur had been his identity since his teens.

The cool I had kept earlier this morning came in handy now. My first thought was to accept that this deal may not close. It would be a mess, but we would still be okay. I had recently launched a CEO peer group in Richmond, Virginia, and had a dozen clients I could continue to coach. I also had two investment banking clients in Virginia. Róbert could still take the job with KPMG or another firm. It would take a couple years longer to establish ourselves, but it would all work out.

Having put these thoughts out of the way, I dedicated my attention to listening to János and Tímea. I reassured them that they did not have to do the deal and that we could pull out, with moderate penalties. What mattered was that János makes what he feels is the right decision for himself and his family. Róbert and I had negotiated the best deal we could do, but there was no telling whether Gramex could grow further under János's management and whether he should hold out and sell it for a better price later.

After about an hour of seller's remorse, János calmed down, reconnected with his original motivations to sell the business, and was ready to move forward. By midday, all the documents had been signed, sealed, and delivered. Róbert and I got our deliverances, too.

WHAT DOES IT TAKE TO DO IT?

Going through with a transaction is a physically, mentally, and emotionally taxing process. It is not unlike a pregnancy, in its length, growing intensity, ups and downs, and the painful yet cathartic finale. The analogy is only partially accurate, because a baby cannot stay unborn. The sale of a small-to-medium-size business often falls through for various reasons: One or both parties may change their mind, the parties can't compromise, the economy may tank, or the money dries up.

If you have followed the steps laid out in this book so far, you now have a self-managing, fast-growing, highly profitable—in one word, Buyable—business you can fully or partially sell or recapitalize. But you still have to accomplish a well-run sales process.

Your Three Jobs During the Transaction

Prepare to invest 12 to 18 months in the sale process for your business. You might complete the transaction in half that time, but it would be the exception that proves the rule. You want to have enough time to resist rushing into half-cooked compromises.

As mentioned earlier, you have three important jobs during the sale process:

1. Hire and empower an M&A advisor, also called investment banker, that you can trust.
2. Show up when your banker needs you to sell buyers on your vision for the business.
3. Keep pressing on the accelerator to make sure your business's growth doesn't stall during the transaction process.

Find an M&A advisor who knows your industry, has good references, is a strategic thinker, believes in the potential of your business, and is someone you can get along with. Make sure they have a competent team, too: At least two people who can relieve the lead banker from administrative duties so that person can focus on strategy, tactics, and communications.

Pick a firm that is the right size for your company. If your business is bigger than the deals the banking firm has done in the past, it may struggle to command respect with buyers and their advisors. If you're at the lower end of its deal scale, you may slip off the priority list. The sweet spot is for your business to be one of the top three of your banker's clients.

When you have hired the right banker, follow their advice. Choose someone who you can respect and don't feel compelled to second guess. There is no greater boost for an M&A advisor than to have a respectful client that backs them up. Team with your banker and let the partnering avail itself of both of your strengths. Don't let buyers drive a wedge between you because this would only isolate you and make you vulnerable.

THE TRANSACTION

Conducting a sale or capital-raising transaction is a highly structured and administratively intensive process, interspersed with short creative acts that will help you differentiate your business, attract investor interest, and push negotiations over inevitable humps. It typically takes six to nine months to conduct the sale of a Buyable Business. For less buyable ones, the process can take two to three years. In exceptional situations, transactions can be completed much faster, sometimes in a matter of days, but these events are so rare that they aren't worth discussing in this book.

The main steps in the process involve preparing an information memorandum (book) and a teaser that promote the opportunity, attract buyers and bids, share information with qualified bidders so that they can refine and firm up their offers, and negotiate detailed contracts governing risk sharing and, in the case of a partial sale or capital raise, the seller's cohabitation with investing parties.

Figure 11.1 shows the steps leading up to a transaction.

Figure 11.1 The Process of Selling Your Business or Raising Capital

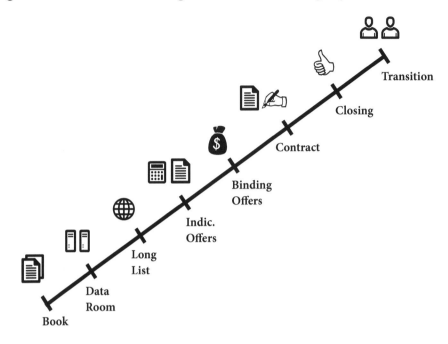

PREPARATION

The right banker will immerse themselves in your business. The product of this immersion is an information memorandum or "book," which is an in-depth sales presentation of your business.

The Book

The book serves three purposes:

1. It establishes the credibility and professionalism of the seller and the seller's management team.
2. It presents a compelling money-making opportunity to the generic buyer.
3. It identifies and manages all potential objections that buyers may think of.

Your investment banker will build your book in the shape of an inverted pyramid. At the tip of the pyramid, it starts with an executive summary that makes the business case for an investment into your business and how the buyer would make money.

Then the banker backs up each statement made in the business case with detailed and credible proof. The book stakes out the vision for your company, how it will continue to be successful, exploiting opportunities with manageable risks by using its existing resources, independent of any buyers'.

The book must also show a clear and consistent picture of your business's financial statements and it often includes financial projections that help the buyer visualize the opportunity. Buyers scrutinize the past to learn how good are your business and its management. But they are buying the future and the stream of profits that your company will generate after a transaction.

The job of the M&A advisor is to elevate the image of your company by projecting professionalism and dedication and by helping you convey an enticing vision of a promising future. This is especially necessary when you're leaving the business because, when your Next Chapter is not set to unfold in the business, you will no longer see the company's future since it will have nothing to do with you anymore. Your future may be playing golf, starting another business, traveling, or supporting charitable causes, but it is no longer building this company. Without a banker who brings the curiosity and desire to visualize a credible future for the business, you are severely limiting the opportunity being offered.

When I was selling the logistics software business Tellogen to a Polish buyer, we projected Tellogen's vast expansion into the Central and Eastern European transportation markets, which dovetailed with the buyer group's ambition to become a pan-regional software group. For toy distributor Gulliver, we projected a geographic expansion to neighboring Romania. For contract researchers Goodwill Research, we predicted growth into neighboring countries and into performing Phase 1 drug trials for other entities of its Italian suitor.

Your banker then summarizes the book in a one-page document called the teaser. The teaser leads with a curiosity-inducing headline and gives prospective buyers an executive summary of the opportunity. It masks your company's identity so that buyers can't identify your business until they have signed a nondisclosure agreement (NDA).

Data Room

Before inviting investors to review the opportunity, you must have a data room compiled that includes all the information investors need to make a committed offer. Preparing the data room early helps you discover any flaws in your company's compliance, risk management, and reporting before prospective buyers do. The premium version of the data room is called vendor due diligence (VDD).

Best done by a Big Four or second-tier accounting firm, a VDD is a mock due diligence review that helps ferret out and fix any financial, environmental, IP protection, documentation, tax optimization, employment, legal, and regulatory compliance issues. By the time buyers show up, their own due diligence review should be merely a formality because your company has already discovered and corrected all issues, leaving investors no opportunity or excuse to reduce their offer. Having a VDD done reduces the cost for bidders and attracts more potential buyers to the table. When a trustworthy, leading CPA firm prepares the VDD, buyers accept much of the findings.

The downside of the VDD is that CPAs charge you multiple five figures for it, and sometimes more. A less expensive but also less credible alternative is to have your M&A advisor help you compile the data room.

During the sale of Goodwill Research, a $5 million sales revenue business, we hired our own Big Four–trained CPA, who cleaned up nearly all the gaps in documentation and unusual practices before the Italian buyer's Big Four accountants showed up. Compiling the data room was a monumental task, requiring multiple all-nighters to finish on time. Thankfully, the effort bore fruit, because our buyer accepted the file.

214

Buyer List

While part of the team or external accountants are working on populating a solid data room, the investment banker researches a wide list of potential buyers and investors for your company, including the following:

- Local and international peers and competitors
- Large public and private companies that operate in adjacent segments
- Local and international private equity buyers
- Family offices targeting this type of company
- Potential buy-in executives who could augment the management team and attract private equity money
- Acquisitive conglomerates
- Major vendors and customers
- Companies that sell to the same customers
- Platform companies of private equity groups

Companies like Amadeus, owned by Moody's, offer subscriptions to their databases, which contain data on more than 350 million private European companies, including financial, leadership, and transaction-related information. In the United States, Infogroup and Dun & Bradstreet provide similar information for buyer research. If you're looking for financial buyers and corporate acquirers, check out Intralinks' Deal Sourcing Network and Axial.net.

The aim is to identify all possible buyers and then narrow the list to a couple hundred companies that have the financial strength to buy your business and that are a potential strategic fit.

The next step is to prioritize buyers. It is best to start with large strategic acquirers because they can afford to write the biggest checks, even if they are often much slower to react than private equity groups. It is worth giving the strategics a few weeks of advance notice so they can issue indicative offers around the same time as do private equity funds, which can respond to attractive opportunities in real time.

It is impossible to know with certainty which buyers will bite. It depends on their current acquisition strategy (which can shift rapidly from hot to cold), their deal-making capacity, motivation, experiences, affinity with your type of target, and the individual running the takeover department. You can realize a major advantage when buyers know your advisor as a source of quality deals. Because CEOs are anxious to avoid wasting time with undetermined sellers and unattractive companies, they prefer deals from bankers they know and have found reliable.

One of the best ways to identify buyers is to know people and uncover opportunities that aren't obvious, but that are tailormade for your company. MB Partners sold several businesses that way, including these:

- A contractor that builds renewable energy plants to an industrial conglomerate six months after a chance chat with the CEO about the conglomerate's interest in the energy sector.
- A company that heat-treats car brakes to the retired former CEO of a publicly traded automotive business, who was itching to get back into the game. The deal was funded by a tech company that we knew was trying to create a positive narrative away from its core business of adult entertainment.
- A distributor of wheelchairs and other rehabilitation-linked medical products in Hungary to the manufacturer of orthopedic shoes in Poland.

After researching the buyer list, it is time to line up indicative offers from investors.

FINDING YOUR INVESTOR

Indicative Offers

Your M&A advisor will send potential buyers who expressed interest a one- or two-page teaser that describes the investment opportunity and an

NDA, which buyers must sign before receiving the book. The investment banker's job is to coordinate interested parties in such a way that as many as possible issue indicative bids for the business. A successful process creates competitive tension and infects buyers with deal fever, leading to aggressive bids.

The opposite is also true. If there are only a handful of buyers, they often sense a lack of competition and quickly lose interest or make lowball offers. One tactic buyers use in low-competition situations is to demand exclusivity so they can take control of the process and negotiate from a position of strength. Exclusivity often becomes a one-way street when the buyer keeps dangling a carrot while dragging out the process, bleeding out the hapless seller, who is already distracted by the sale of the company and is no longer focusing on running the business.

Rushing It Through a Closing Window

In 2008, we represented Botond, the owner of Tisatela, a regional internet service provider (ISP). Botond saw that his business was about to peak, and he decided to sell it before it was too late. We approached a cable TV consolidator, "Opticweb," that made an offer for Tisatela alongside two other bidders and started due diligence in late summer. Soon after, Lehman Brothers went belly up, triggering the global financial crisis, and all mergers and acquisitions deal activity dried up immediately. Opticweb, too, slammed on the brakes.

It looked like Tisatela had missed its window of opportunity to sell when Opticweb reemerged in November and made an offer that was 40 percent lower than its initial, seller-approved offer. When Botond accepted it, the Opticweb team told him they wanted exclusivity and pressured him to fire MB Partners and negotiate without advisors. We advised him to go along because decreasing internet subscription prices and spiking customer churn were about to break Tisatela's growth momentum, which could push Botond's exit back for at least 18 months and possibly indefinitely.

We continued to support him feverishly from the background and eventually attended final negotiations the day before Christmas. Tisatela had practically no cards left to play, and Botond was conceding most of the final terms of the contract. The two parties signed the deal in the wee hours of December 23 and closed before the New Year. In January, the bottom fell out of the ISP market and it turned out that Botond had sold Tisatela at a high multiple based on its eventual 2009 earnings.

Binding Offers

Bidders make indicative offers when they like what they read in the book and see on the ground when they visit the business and its management. Buyers that have qualified themselves by submitting decent indicative bids are then allowed to proceed to the next stage and confirm that everything they read in the book and heard from management is correct. If they discover any gaps, they can state them.

Buyers are allowed a set time to conduct their due diligence audits and management team interviews, after which they can submit a *binding offer* that includes a firm purchase price and payment terms, subject to contract.

Sometimes a seller is not in the position to dictate the terms of a sale. For example, when there are only a handful of potential buyers; when the business has weaknesses that the seller knows would require friendlier seller–buyer talks to handle, such as environmental issues or pending litigations; or when the business is in a narrow niche or is too small for corporate or private equity buyers.

In such circumstances the seller might agree to a mutual exclusivity agreement with a preferred bidder by signing a letter of intent. An LOI gives the buyer one to three months, sometimes longer, to negotiate a deal bilaterally. The longer the exclusivity period, the less chance the seller has to invite other buyers to the table and improve its negotiating position. LOIs are typically agreed at the indicative offer stage, alleviating the need for a binding offer round because there are no longer other competing parties for the seller to choose from. The exception is when the buyer initiates a negative adjustment to the price and terms, which gives the seller an opportunity to terminate negotiations with the preferred bidder and reopen talks with others. In practice this is rare because if there were multiple competing offers, the seller would likely not have agreed to an LOI in the first place.

By following the recipe in this book, you will have built a Buyable Business that should have no problem attracting multiple competitive bids.

Auction to a Single Buyer

Controlling the sale process is critical to creating competitive tension and improving the price and terms of a sale. Your M&A advisor will do their best to canvass all possible buyers and maximize interest at the indicative offer stage. If there are multiple strong bidders, the seller team can exude confidence, which is proof to buyers that the target is hot. This translates into increased bids and more lenient terms for the seller.

However, when only a single buyer is interested (or a handful), it can kill confidence on both sides. The lower confidence saps motivation or triggers an opportunistic attitude in the few buyers. They will want to maneuver themselves into an exclusive situation and exploit any weaknesses as a pretext to negotiating the price down, spreading out payments over time, and passing the risk of future profitability to the seller.

In such situations, the seller's only leverage is to threaten walking away from the deal, a tactic the seller is not always willing or able to use without losing credibility. Some sellers make bombastic statements or issue empty threats, which can backfire on them. It is imperative that you rustle up multiple buyers for your business or maintain that impression with the buyer you do have.

In 2006, we negotiated the sale of electrical contractor Epsillon and found only a single reliable bidder, the Dutch Janzzen Group. The group made a reasonable offer, but the seller, Solt, wanted to push for a higher price and told Janzzen that we had received a higher offer, which was untrue. The buyer thanked us for the opportunity and said he could wait. Solt's bluff weakened our position because we had to go back to Janzzen hat in hand one month later to rekindle discussions at the lower price Solt was then ready to accept. The result was a dragged-out contract negotiation and a significant amount of money left in escrow for a period of years.

We would have been better off negotiating a brief exclusivity period based on Janzzen's offer and pushing for a fast deal closing at the threat of "bringing other buyers to the table." Janzzen could not have been sure whether we had competing offers, which would have kept us more in control, yielding more lenient contract terms.

In another deal, we represented a regional ISP called Kaposweb. We found only a handful of obvious buyers, none of which came through. However, we received a surprise last-minute offer from a regional competitor, TKH.

TKH's offer turned out to be the only acceptable one we received, and we fretted as its acquisition team put up a show of being savvy operators and ruthless negotiators. However, the seller was a street-smart entrepreneur and spotted the insecurity behind their posturing. He suggested that we should call their bluff.

We refused the exclusivity TKH asked for and held the buyer to an aggressive timetable during which it had to wrap up its due diligence and issue a binding offer within weeks. TKH took the bait and even increased its offer in the second round to win the "auction." The deal closed in record time and yielded top dollar for our client.

This tactic is difficult to pull off because it requires a delicate judgment of the balance of the various forces that are in operation at the same time, and a dose of luck. We were helped by having a fearless client and an eager buyer that used bluster to try to hide its inexperience. The tactic could have exposed us if TKH had missed our deadline and we had to soften our process to accommodate it, as happened with Solt in the Janzzen deal above.

Auction to a single buyer works best when you have a short window of opportunity to do the deal and have nothing to lose by putting pressure to close on your only bidder. MB Partners worked on a transaction where the 29-year-old owner of an electronics retailer tasked us with selling his business before his thirtieth birthday so he could fulfill his childhood dream of becoming a millionaire in his twenties. We were racing against the clock and could play hard-to-get with a single bidder. In this case the deal failed to close on time and our client decided to keep the business for another decade.

With a binding offer in hand, the transaction can move into the endgame.

THE ENDGAME

Contract Negotiations

After a binding offer is made, the seller typically selects the preferred bidder with which to conduct the final negotiations of the sale and purchase agreement.

With a partial sale or recapitalization, a shareholder agreement is next to be negotiated. The buyer's aim at this point is to minimize its risk by negotiating representations, warranties, and indemnities, which are typically secured by part of the purchase price and held out of reach of the seller in escrow for an agreed time.

I have seen anything from a 10 percent escrow for three months to a 40 percent escrow for four years. Buyers concerned about the management transition often buy only a 51 percent controlling stake first, with a put and call option for the remaining shares over a three-year period. A put option allows the seller to sell and the call option permits the buyer to buy the remaining shares of the seller after an agreed time period and at a pre-agreed price formula. A gradual deal like this reduces the buyer's risk of finding and grooming a successor CEO as well as the risk of overpaying for the acquisition by purchasing the remaining 49 percent at a multiple of future profits.

Bleeding the Seller to Death

Some buyers, when they sense a seller has burned bridges, drag their feet until they push the hapless business owner to the point of despair, ready to quit in disgust.

At one time, MB Partners represented a young entrepreneur, Hugo, who had created a fast-growing distributor of GPS devices. Unfortunately, the business borrowed heavily to finance its growing receivables balance and inventories. Hugo's firm got caught with its pants down when GPS device sales slowed with the rise of smartphone-based GPS applications.

The business was still doing okay when we found a Norwegian strategic buyer who was interested in acquiring the markets and management team of Hugo's company. The potential buyer made powerful statements about its buying intentions to motivate the seller while delaying a financial commitment. As Hugo's advisors, we were forced to negotiate with the buyer's CEO, Noah, while the owner, Malthe, held all the cards.

The deal started out as a purchase of the original business, which, however, ran out of cash. Hugo continued the business in a new legal entity across the border in Slovakia. He hoped that the acquisition would happen and registered his new company in the name of the buyer's holding entity. This smelled of desperation and further strengthened the buyer's hand.

Finally, early the following year, we pinned Noah down and scheduled final negotiations and contract signing in Budapest. For this meeting, Malthe also showed up, and in his boss's presence, Noah was finally under pressure to deliver the deal. Hugo and I turned the table on him and dragged out the talks well into the night. We got them to give up more than 50 percent of the negotiating ground they had forced us to concede over the previous six months. Noah and Malthe were furious and MB Partners was uninvited from the closing dinner.

Buyers routinely apply hardball tactics against entrepreneurs. You need strong advisors who can protect you in such situations.

Signing and Closing the Deal

The sale of a company is not final until the cash clears the bank. This often happens on the day of signing the contracts, but sometimes the closing is delayed by contingencies. These could include the audit of year-end financial statements, confirmation that the seller has registered patents and trademarks, and clearance from antitrust authorities that the combination doesn't restrict competition.

The trouble with delayed closings is that a dramatic change in the economy or in the business can make the buyer run. Solt had to wait two months for the Epsillon deal to close because of a formal antitrust process.

Sometimes the closing falls through on the last day. This almost happened with the Goodwill Research transaction, when the Italians showed up at the signing table with a shocking last-minute demand of deferring 20 percent of the purchase price contingent on the next year's financial performance.

The deal that did fall through at the signing table was the sale of Struktoor (see the full story in Chapter 1), when the seller's CEO demanded a 50 percent pay raise from his prospective new employers. Because Sasha had already changed the terms three times previously, this ultimatum proved to be the last drop in the bucket and killed the deal.

Closing deals is an art as much as a science. It requires the balancing of savvy negotiations with the building of trust between the two parties. You can only push your counterpart so far before destroying the trust that is eventually required to bridge the gap on a handful of compromises that keep both of you somewhat exposed to the other after the transaction. This is why it is important to find negotiating parties that can relate to each other. Recall Elias, the gray-haired executive who was brought in to negotiate with the fellow engineer owners of GAJ with whom he shared a profession and an age group. It also helps to choose a transaction attorney who matches the profile of the buyer's legal team.

Your investment banker should be able to build credibility with buyers at a personal level. I often helped diffuse the anger of buyers and my own clients when they misinterpreted each other's actions and reactions in tense situations by providing context to the thinking of the other party.

Following the signing and closing of the sale, the next milestone is the management transition.

Management Transition

Transitioning the management team to the new owner can be a short process if the company is already self-managing or when the buyer brings in its own management team. Gulliver had great transition processes: The buyer recruited an industry veteran to run the business and was thus willing to release Csaba three months after closing. With the PartsCo sale, there was no inside management to speak of, but the incoming CEO knew the industry and the main customers and was comfortable taking over from the outgoing owner right away.

When a buyer goes into a transaction without a management team to install, it often needs two to five years to find the seller's successor and will then have to groom that person or team. We helped the owner of a frozen pastry manufacturer recruit a CEO, who cohabitated with him for 18 months before the transaction, allowing the founder to leave right after the closing.

In most cases, when a buyer has to rely on the seller to manage the business, it defers part of the purchase price in the form of an earn-out to be paid in line with how the business performs during the transition. By the time of the payout, the buyer is in charge of financial controls and hiring auditors, and this often results in disputes and litigation about the amount of earn-out payable to the seller.

Sometimes negotiating the earn-out formula becomes so contentious that the buyer acquires 100 percent of the stock on closing to ensure it has full flexibility to manage the business during the transition. This lets the seller off the hook regarding future company performance. In the wake of such decisions, the buyers lost out in both the Goodwill Research and the Tellogen deals discussed earlier.

The seeds of harmonious or contentious cohabitations are sowed during the negotiation process—another reason for both parties to focus on building trust and negotiating the transaction in good faith, using sound arguments. An entrepreneur will only function well as part of the buyer entity if they can trust the acquirer to treat them fairly and if they can be trusted in return.

KEY IDEAS

- Your three jobs during a transaction are to: (1) hire and empower an M&A advisor you trust, (2) show up when your advisor needs you to sell buyers on your vision for the business, and (3) ensure your business's growth doesn't stall during the transaction process.

- Preparation for the deal includes preparing a book, a data room, and a buyers list.
- Finding your buyer consists of researching all strategic, private equity, family office, and management buy-in investors. Then you send them a one-page teaser and ask them to sign an NDA to access a copy of the book. This is followed by a buyer due diligence performed by a leading CPA firm, which is sometimes replaced by a vendor due diligence. Interested acquirers make a binding offer for the business.
- The seller chooses the best offeror as a preferred bidder for negotiations. Strong companies can negotiate harder than marginal ones.
- Keep alert during the transaction. It is not over until the cash has cleared the bank and all indemnities have been lifted.

(12)

LIVE YOUR PURPOSE

SAYING GOODBYE

After I spent one year commuting between Richmond, Budapest, and Bucharest, selling MB Partners and simplifying my life came as a relief. I was sick of leaving my family every three weeks, living out of suitcases, suffering jet lag. The worst thing was that I was often working around the clock because of the geographic challenges. By the time Róbert and I would get home from our office in Richmond, Cosmin, who ran the Bucharest office, was arriving at his desk. I woke up each morning to a flood of emails.

Still, letting go of my business was emotionally hard, and it left a void in me. I had hired every employee in that company and liked and respected each of them. We fused together as a team through the pains and exhilarations, disappointments and triumphs of working in a fast-moving, volatile business. What was life going to be like without MB Partners?

The reality of the change hit me as soon as Krisztián, the buyer, and I shook hands after signing the sale of my company. Oriens Group arranged a team dinner for that evening—to which I was not invited. My friends were suddenly playing on the opposing team.

Krisztián Orbán, Oriens Group, and I shake hands upon the sale of MB Partners.

With MB Partners sold, gone was part of my identity of being a recognized dealmaker in town, and my face disappeared from the cover of the industry-leading periodical *Cégérték*, which was hitting 2,500 entrepreneurial mailboxes each month.

What blunted my pain was that I still owned the fledgling Bucharest office, run by Cosmin Mizof, and our Richmond branch, where Róbert János Nagy had joined me to work on the Gramex deal and to service our clients in Virginia. Without the unsold remnants of my firm in Romania and Virginia and the excitement of making it in America, selling MB Partners would have been much harder still.

Why Exits Are Hard

I don't care how talented you are, you will not build a Buyable Business without being invested in it. That often means working 60- to 80-hour weeks for 10 or 15 years. Entrepreneurship crowds out hobbies and much of the time that other people spend on their social life and family. By the time you build a valuable business, it has become part of who you are, if not most of your identity.

What is difficult about leaving, then, is that you're not just exiting a business but also upending your life. Imagine if Itzhak Perlman could no longer play the violin but only the piano or the flute. Or if Lionel Messi was not allowed to play or coach soccer but only other sports like basketball and hockey. Or if Paul McCartney had a noncompete and could no longer write songs but had to write novels or paint instead.

So, how can you overcome this loss? Are there alternatives?

First, you may not have to sell your company. The key point of building a Buyable Business is that you create a valuable asset that you can turn into wealth even without a sale. The only reason to sell is if you have a more interesting future planned outside of your business other than being its owner. If you need more money for your Next Chapter than you can extract from the business without its sale, consider building that higher value over a longer time horizon.

Creating a successful business is one of the greatest adventures you can experience. Building and growing MB Partners was the most exciting period of my life. Why stop the adventure early if you still have a desire to contribute? You may decide to keep the business but reposition your role in it so it fits your ideal lifestyle. As long as you control the company and find competent management to run it, you can choose any role you want that suits you. Fiat's Gianni Agnelli remained honorary chairman of his company until his death at the ripe old age of 82.

Many of my clients ended up regretting the decision to sell early, and several of them started another company as soon as their noncompete expired, sometimes earlier, behind the scenes.

The smart ones found something else that kept them engaged inside the company or outside of it. Let's review your options if you want to stay engaged with your business after the sale.

STAYING ENGAGED

Staying On as an Advisor

After selling MB Partners, I stayed on another year as an advisor. We had to make sure that all clients transitioned and were happy under the new ownership, and I had a stake in completing a handful of transactions, so I wanted to monitor them. My assignment lasted 12 months, and I faded out toward the end.

Gino Wickman, the creator of the Entrepreneurial Operating System, continues to act as an advisor to EOS Worldwide, which he sold to a private equity group in 2018. Gino, who still owns part of the company, shows up at EOS-organized conferences to reassure employees and licensees. He has since started another business but continues to keynote special events and act as an elder statesman for the company.

Continuing as CEO

Another option to stay engaged with your company is to continue managing the business. Most buyers prefer to have the seller hang around until a suitable replacement is found and transitioned in.

Solt stayed on as CEO for four more years after selling Epsillon. He did as good a job as could be expected of an entrepreneur in a corporate environment. He took time off for travels and family, but he returned to business and started a similar venture after his noncompete agreement expired.

A Richmond entrepreneur, Jeff Marks, sold Promotional Considerations, a business he started in 1984, to Vanguard Industries in 2006. He stayed on as a hired-hand president and chief salesperson until in 2018 Vanguard offered him the chance to repurchase the company. He returned as the owner of the business he founded, but two years later he sold it again, this time to a Virginia-based strategic buyer. He agreed to run the business for a two-year transition period.

Staying for a few years to run the business can be a good way to phase yourself out if the buyers stay relatively hands-off during that period. When this doesn't happen, then founders leave: Entrepreneurs don't like to be managed by corporate bureaucrats.

Staying On as a Minority Investor

Warren Buffett created the model of making permanent investments alongside strong founders. This scheme has been widely adopted by family offices not bound by investment time frames like private equity funds are. The latter keep portfolio companies for three to seven years, after which they must exit and return the funds raised to investors.

On the other hand, gaining "perpetual" investors enables founders to diversify the wealth they have tied up in the business and maintain quasi-entrepreneurial autonomy, as long as their financial partners don't meddle.

However, I have rarely seen founders stick around with strategic buyers in minority positions. Two former clients I've mentioned, the founder of Goodwill Research and that of Tellogen, soon became unhappy with taking orders from their paid bosses and got out. Few entrepreneurs, after gaining financial independence, put up with corporate life and with others, especially nonowners, making decisions over their heads.

Become a Specialist in the Business

Another Richmond entrepreneur is Gary LeClair, who cofounded a fast-growing law firm in 1988. Over the next 23 years, LeClairRyan expanded nationwide and at its peak had 21 offices. Gary ran the business as a corporation CEO and built a management team around him, to which he gradually delegated the running of the firm. By early 2011, he stepped down as CEO and went back to work on venture capital deals, his professed love.

Epilogue: After Gary gave up the CEO reins, LeClairRyan's competitiveness eroded and key partners left, including, eventually, Gary. In September 2019, the board closed down the firm.

I've heard many entrepreneurs fantasize about it, but I have yet to see any other example of a founder successfully working as a contributor in the business after stepping down. Even Gary's case ended with an eventual exit.

Take a C-Level Position

Another option is to stay involved in management without top-level responsibility.

Péter, cofounder and director of sales and procurement of the Gulliver toy company, stuck around after the sale of the business. He kept his C-level position, while the private equity buyer recruited a new CEO to run the company. Péter was not as engaged in the ice hockey community as was his friend Csaba and decided that selling his shares was no reason to give up a job he enjoyed and was good at.

Entrepreneurs who find fulfillment working in a business that they have grown and sold are rare. If you give up control to anyone outside of your own family, you are better off looking for your future purpose outside of the business.

Only sell your business if you have something more exciting waiting for you as your Next Chapter. Retirement is not a goal in itself. Think about what is worth retiring to.

If you're like Richard Branson, you can hand over the management of your business and focus on the pieces you enjoy, such as starting and acquiring new businesses or working on strategy. These activities can take up as much or as little of your time as you want.

You may best enjoy creating new businesses, preferring to hand them over to independent management as soon as the baby is walking and has learned to speak. You may not want more than a handful of entrepreneurial people to manage, and that's okay.

You may prefer to use the money you made with your original business to invest in your passion outside of it, like Charles Saatchi did. He collects art, but other entrepreneurs collect cars, buy wineries, or help other people by starting or funding nonprofits.

You may just want to take a long sabbatical, like Solt did, travel for a few years and watch the kids grow up and then start another business in your own field. If your buyer failed with your business, or if its corporate strategy shifted, it might be happy to sell the business back to you. This happens a lot more often than most people realize.

Others, like Jack Welch, want to share their wisdom through public speaking and occasional consulting. Having built a successful business, you have learned a lot and now have the time to teach it. Even if your competitors know as much as you do, they may still be busy applying that knowledge, and you can be the one documenting your journey and leaving the legacy in your industry.

When Winston Churchill lost the general election after winning World War II, he became the first protagonist to write the story of the war, and his version became the dominant narrative. It also won him a Nobel Prize.

Or you may just want to retire to spend time with your family and friends, which can make for a great Next Chapter. Both of my grandfathers enjoyed long retirements crammed with social and intellectual activities and they seemed happy and fulfilled. That may just be your ticket too.

The only thing that matters is to be intentional and to consider what the future can offer. Find a purpose that excites you, that you look forward to, before you pull the trigger on selling your business.

KEY IDEAS

- Exits can be difficult and sometimes anticlimactic. Develop an exciting purpose beyond your business before you give up control of it.
- If you stay, pick a role you are comfortable with, and let go of trying to control ownership decisions.
- You may keep your Buyable Business and transition to become CEO, a

C-level executive, advisor, minority investor, or even a specialist in the business. Your success chiefly depends on your relationship with the new owner, who will henceforth make the decisions. Most entrepreneurs end up leaving eventually.

- Don't sell until you have figured out your Next Chapter, a purpose in life that will make you at least as happy and fulfilled as owning a successful business did.

CONCLUSION

If you don't know where you're going, you might end up someplace else.

—YOGI BERRA

Sasha and Ace, the owners of Struktoor, built a successful business, but they had no clear financial or lifestyle goals and their company ended up in bankruptcy as they landed in prosecution.

Contrast them with the founders of Gulliver, who had a plan and systematically built a Buyable Business. All four of them realized their post-deal goals: Krisztina conquered the Arctic and the Antarctic, and Csaba led the Hungarian national hockey team to play in the Elite Division of the World Hockey Championships. Péter stayed on as head of sales and procurement, and Ildikó freed herself up to enjoy her children and grandchildren.

Building a successful business is a special blessing and fantastic experience. You embark on an exhilarating journey—you are making a difference in the lives of hundreds of employees and customers. The secret is to create a Buyable Business with a plan that fits your personality, desires, and aspirations and to execute this plan with tenacity and discipline.

A Buyable Business is a well-built and well-operated organization that is growing and profitable. It gives you options when you're ready to make a change in life. A Buyable Business is also fun to manage or is designed to self-manage.

Begin with the end in mind and decide the future you want so you can design your business to help you achieve it. Proactive business owners create their own luck when it comes time to harvest their Buyable Business, whereas reactive business owners end up losing their business or selling it under pressure at a discount. You therefore need a plan.

Determine the Magic Number that equips you to step into the Next Chapter of your life, be it starting another business, collecting on a retirement nest egg, or gathering capital for philanthropic or hobby endeavors.

Calculate the value you need to create in your business that will allow you to harvest your Magic Number. Consider the growth rate you must generate over your time horizon, and adjust the time horizon or your goals if necessary.

Then grow your business using one of the 10 Management Blueprints. These generic franchise systems package the management concepts that successful corporations have used since the publication of *The Principles of Scientific Management* in 1911. When you understand The Seven Management Concepts, you can choose the right Management Blueprint to grow your business.

EOS and other Management Blueprints provide the tools you need to create alignment, execute with discipline, and foster a positive culture that you can sustain. Your blueprint shows you how to build a solid foundation to save money, increase the potential value of your business, and create luck for yourself. It's as simple as following a proven process.

Act like a professional investor and engineer value drivers into your business so you create the highest value in the shortest time. When you reach the point when your business is functioning optimally, groom the business to make the best impression on potential buyers and investors and to reap the best offers.

In the course of building your Buyable Business, you will consider what is important to you when cashing in on your company. You can pick the path that works for you both financially and emotionally and that fits your lifestyle and purpose.

It is imperative you have an interesting future waiting for you after the sale of your business and that you have realistic expectations about your relationship to your company if you give up control.

Follow the Buyable framework and you will build a self-managing and highly valuable business that you can decide to keep or sell.

I wish you a rewarding, exhilarating, and fulfilling journey.

ABOUT THE AUTHOR

 **STEVE PREDA's** "Why" is to help entrepreneurs reach their ideal lives while building a great business. He believes that with the right tools and coaching we can eradicate "Business Covid" in America, and save 185,000 companies each year from disappearing.

Steve built and sold an investment banking firm in Europe before moving to the United States in 2012. Since then, he has helped thousands of businesses grow their teams, revenues, and profits as an author, speaker, coach, and as the founder of Steve Preda Business Growth (SPBG).

Steve explores business-growth shortcuts on the Management Blueprint podcast, and he and his fellow SPBG Guides™ love helping growth-minded entrepreneurs and their leadership teams reach their business-pinnacles.

Read Steve's other books, including, Pinnacle: Five Principles that Take Your Business to the Top of the Mountain (with Greg Cleary) and Strategy OS: Implement an Advanced Business Operating System in Six Simple Steps.

REVIEW REQUEST

Thanks for reading! If you enjoyed this book or found it useful, I'd be grateful if you'd post a short review on Amazon. Your support really does make a difference, and because I will read all the reviews, I'll be able to get your feedback and make this book even better for a possible future edition.

Thanks again for your support!

Steve Preda

ACKNOWLEDGMENTS

I have poured the last twenty years of my life into this book and I could not have succeeded without a fantastic group of people who walked with me for part or for this entire journey.

The writing of this book could not have happened without the inspiration of my dad, Dr. István Préda, who wrote and published several books of his own and with his peers. His example helped me believe that I could one day follow in his footsteps. My beloved wife Dora, and our kids, Emilia, Paula, Istvan, and Sandor, as well as my mom Beáta and sister Katalin encouraged and cheered me along the way.

I owe a debt of gratitude to David Quick, who as my friend coached and nudged me to give this project a go in the wake of the pandemic. He gave me my first start as a speaker and our conversations helped shape the trajectory of this book.

The writing itself could not have gained momentum without the support of the Scribe Writers Room and specifically my writing coaches, Tucker Max, Hal Clifford and Emily Gindlesparger. They gave me the recipe for writing and self-editing this book, and coached me in the initial phase of the project. Bennett Coles, of Cascadia Author Services, has also contributed invaluable guidance.

I was blessed to have been introduced to my wonderful editor Christina Palaia. Christina took a personal interest in helping make *Buyable* much better than I could ever produce on my own. My proofreader Barry Lyons added the thoroughness and precision needed to finalize the manuscript.

In designing the book, I initially relied on Zoltán Ember, who has helped me with all my graphic design needs for the last quarter century and who was joined by cover designer extraordinaire, Jason Anscombe, and the talented illustrator and book designer, Iram Allam. They understood what I wanted and managed to translate my vision into a look and feel I could not be happier with.

Buyable includes a handful of companion online tools that will help you apply the Buyability concepts of the book to your own business and personal situation. I am indebted to Yasser Hawas, who helped me translate these into digital form, using Zoltán Ember's designs.

This book would have been drier and less credible without the real-life stories from many of my current and past clients who permitted me to tell their stories using their real names. I am grateful to Csaba and Ildikó Kovács, Péter and Krisztina Kovalcsik, Zoltán, József and Attila Szabadics, János and Tímea Gréczi, Ottó Skorán, Krisztián Orbán, Heinan Landa, David Campbell, Matt Clark, Jeff Marks, Gary LeClair, Linda Nash, Ethan Giffin, Chris Grandpre and Jeremy Ford for their generosity.

I could not have written this book without my current and former business partners at MB Partners, who helped me build the business and several of whom worked hands-on with me to realize the multiple business preparation and sale transactions mentioned here. Róbert János Nagy, Péter Huncsik, Levente Almási, László Papp, Cosmin Mizof, János Szathmáry, Dániel Mendelényi, Zoltán Szántó and Zoltán Bozó, I owe each of you a debt of gratitude for your partnership and support.

Along the way, I was helped by my friends who kept believing in my journey and stayed by my side over the past quarter century: Csaba "Chubi" Polacsek, Konrád "Mackó" Siegler, Ákos Kiss, Csaba Molnár, Tamas Gal, Greg Waller, Arvin Delgado and Andras "Béró" Feher. Bécó, who recently partook in a Silicon Valley software IPO, and I had spent endless hours in the baths of Budapest three decades ago, dreaming about moving to and making it in America. Thanks to all of you guys for your loyalty and friendship.

It all started with being invited to speak to groups of business owners and I am grateful to my former colleagues at Vistage International, who trusted me to address their members and who were willing to mentor me, including Debbie Tyler, Clyde Northrop, Ed Robinson, David Daugherty, Brian Roberts, Mike Tubridy, Amy Gleklen, Tom Parker and Wally Schmader.

I owe specific gratitude to my EOS® coaches: Gino Wickman, Mark O'Donnell, Mike Paton and CJ Dube for their personal coaching, encouragement, and support.

Last but not least, I want to thank my coaching clients and friends in Richmond Virginia who helped me crystalize many of the concepts of *Buyable* and who served as my sounding board. The list includes but is not limited to Shane Burnette, Brian Burnette, Mark Smith, Jeri Turley, Matt Marek, Chris Rutkai, John Dlugokecki, Amanda Huang, Steve Pierce, Mike Broggie, Terry Fink, Matt Williams, Jack Lawson, Glenn Kurtz, Clay Edwards, Kim Mahan, Paul Giambra, Roger Jetton, Richard Schmitzer, Gordy Fox, Ken Felts, Steve Smith, Natalie Garramone, H. Gregory Waller, and David Lionberger.

FURTHER RESOURCES

Steve Preda Business Growth home page: https://StevePreda.com

Buyability Toolkit website: https://BuyableBusiness.com

Istvan Steve Preda: Insights of a Maverick Exit Advisor, The Diary of 12 Years of Investment Banking in Central Europe and the United States (Glen Allen, Amershire Publishing, 2016)

Istvan Steve Preda: Insights of a Maverick Investment Banker, My Lessons for Business Owners About Selling Entrepreneurial Companies in Central Eastern Europe (Glen Allen, Amershire Publishing, 2013)

Management Blueprint Podcast: https://bit.ly/MBPodcastPlaylistYT

Succession Secrets Podcast: https://apple.co/39RBsah

ENDNOTES

Introduction

1   "U.S. Business Search," Data Axle USA, https://leads-app.infousa.com/
UsBusiness/Selections#tab2

2   "Number of Merger and Acquisition Deals in the United States from
2005 to 2019," Statista, https://www.statista.com/statistics/914665/
number-of-ma-deals-usa/

3   Caitlin Kelly, "Know When to Hold 'Em, Know When to Fold 'Em,"
New York Times, February 10, 2005, https://www.nytimes.com/2005/02/10/
business/know-when-to-hold-em-know-when-to-fold-em.html?auth=log-
in-email&login=email; Gene Marks, *Small Business Desk Reference* (New
York: Penguin, 2004).

4   Philipp Hillenbrand, Dieter Kiewell, Rory Miller-Cheevers, Ivan Ostojic,
and Gisa Springer, "Traditional Company, New Businesses: The Pairing
That Can Ensure an Incumbent's Survival," McKinsey & Company, June
28, 2019, https://www.mckinsey.com/industries/oil-and-gas/our-insights/
traditional-company-new-businesses-the-pairing-that-can-ensure-
an-incumbents-survival

5   SBA Office of Advocacy, "Do Economic or Industry Factors Affect
Business Survival?" *Small Business Facts*, June 2012, https://www.sba.gov/
sites/default/files/Business-Survival.pdf

Chapter 1

6   Michael Gerber, *The E-Myth: Why Most Small Businesses Don't Work and
What to Do About It* (New York: Harper & Row, 1986).

7   https://en.wikipedia.org/wiki/H%C5%8Dshi_Ryokan

Chapter 2

8   "In Pictures: Bill Gates' Fortune over the Years," *Forbes*, June 23, 2008, https://www.forbes.com/2008/06/23/gates-net-worth-tech-gates08-cx_af_0623fortune_slide.html#78fff177dd4e

9   Alex Wilhelm, "A Look Back in IPO: Microsoft, the Software Success," *TechCrunch*, August 8, 2017, https://techcrunch.com/2017/08/08/a-look-back-in-ipo-microsoft-the-software-success/

10 Kim S. Nashand, Patrick Thibodeau, and Dominique Deckmyn, "Update: Ballmer Replaces Gates as Microsoft CEO," *Computerworld*, January 14, 2000, https://www.computerworld.com/article/2592550/update--ballmer-replaces-gates-as-microsoft-ceo.amp.html

11 "List of Philanthropists," *Wikipedia*, last modified October 5, 2020, https://en.wikipedia.org/wiki/List_of_philanthropists; Sarah Boseley, "How Bill and Melinda Gates Helped Save 122m Lives—and What They Want to Solve Next," *The Guardian*, February 14, 2017, https://www.theguardian.com/world/2017/feb/14/bill-gates-philanthropy-warren-buffett-vaccines-infant-mortality

12 "List of Wealthiest Charitable Foundations," *Wikipedia*, last modified October 7, 2020, https://en.wikipedia.org/wiki/List_of_wealthiest_charitable_foundations

13 RankingTheWorld, "Top 10 Richest People in the World (1995–2019)," YouTube video, 5:00, March 25, 2019, https://www.youtube.com/watch?v=UkhLvJ6RSKc

14 "Microsoft," *Wikipedia*, last modified October 7, 2020, https://en.wikipedia.org/wiki/Microsoft

15 "Charles Saatchi," *Wikipedia*, last modified August 10, 2020, https://en.wikipedia.org/wiki/Charles_Saatchi

16 "Linda Nash," Linda Nash Ventures, http://lindanashventures.com/wp/who-we-are

17 "Jack Welch," *Wikipedia*, last modified August 23, 2020, https://en.wikipedia.org/wiki/Jack_Welch.

18 Cover Story Behind the Fall of Steve Jobs, CNN Money, August 5, 1985 https://money.cnn.com/magazines/fortune/fortune_archive/1985/08/05/66254/index.htm

19 Mark Morgan Ford, "What's Your Magic Number? Retirement Planning Anyone Can Do," Early to Rise, January 7, 2014, https://www.earlytorise.com/retirement-planning/

20 Dan Sullivan, *My Plan for Living to 156: Imaginatively Extend Your Lifetime to Transform How You Live in the Present* (Toronto: The Strategic Coach, 2018). Cartoons by Hamish MacDonald.

Chapter 3

21   See Pepperdine Graziadio Business School, Private Capital Markets Project, https://bschool.pepperdine.edu/institutes-centers/centers/applied-research/research/pcmsurvey/

22   Craig R. Everett, *2019 Private Capital Markets Report* (Malibu, CA: Pepperdine University Graziadio Business School, March 18, 2019), http://digitalcommons.pepperdine.edu/gsbm_pcm_pcmr/12

23   "Companies Who Joined Vistage over the Past Five Years Grew 2.2× Faster Than Average Small and Medium-Sized U.S. Businesses, According to a 2017 Analysis," Vistage Worldwide, 2017, https://www.vistage.com/wp-content/uploads/2017/06/Vistage-Member-Companies-Proven-Growth.pdf

Chapter 4

24   Gene Landrum, *Entrepreneurial Genius* (Naples, FL: Brendan Kelly Publishing, 2004), chap. 12

25   "Peter F. Drucker: Quotes," Goodreads, https://www.goodreads.com-quotes/375321-your-first-and-foremost-job-as-a-leader-is-to; "Frederick-Winslow Taylor," British Library, https://www.bl.uk/people/frederickwin-slow-taylor; "We Cannot Predict the Future, But We Can Invent It," Quote Investigator, https://quoteinvestigator.com/2012/09/27/ invent-the-future/

26   Walter Isaacson, *Steve Jobs* (New York: Simon & Schuster, 2011).

27   "Andrew Grove," *Wikipedia*, last modified September 8, 2020, https://en.wikipedia.org/wiki/Andrew_Grove

28   What Matters, "What Is an OKR? Andy Grove, OKR Inventor, Explains," YouTube video, 2:26, https://www.youtube.com/watch?time_continue=37&v=1ht_1VAF6ik&feature=emb_logo

29   Richard S. Tedlow, *Andy Grove: The Life and Times of an American Business Icon* (New York: Penguin, 2006).

30   Andy Grove, *Only the Paranoid Survive* (New York: Doubleday, 1996).

31   Adam Lashinsky, "Remembering Andy Grove, Mentor and Defender of Silicon Valley," *Fortune*, March 22, 2016, https://fortune.com/2016/03/22/remembering-andy-grove/

32   James Coates, "Andrew Grove," *Chicago Tribune*, November 3, 1996, https://www.chicagotribune.com/news/ct-xpm-1996-11-03-9611030353-story.html

33   Oliver Staley, "Silicon Valley's Confrontational Management Style Started

with Andy Grove," Quartz, March 22, 2016, https://qz.com/645327/
silicon-valleys-confrontational-management-style-started-with-
andy-grove/

34 "James C. Collins," *Wikipedia*, last modified September 15, 2020,
https://en.wikipedia.org/wiki/James_C._Collins

35 Jim Collins, "Good to Great," Jim Collins, October 2001,
https://www.jimcollins.com/article_topics/articles/good-to-great.html

Chapter 5

36 "The True Failure Rate of Small Businesses," January 3, 2021, https://www.
entrepreneur.com/article/361350.

38 Now SRC Holding Corporation.

38 "SRC Remanufacturing History & Culture," SRC, https://www.srcreman.
com/history-and-culture.

39 "Springfield ReManufacturing," *Wikipedia*, last modified January 29, 2020,
https://en.wikipedia.org/wiki/Springfield_ReManufacturing

40 Jack Stack, "Introduction," in *The Great Game of Business* (New York:
Currency Doubleday, 1992).

41 Verne Harnish, *Mastering the Rockefeller Habits*, 1st ed. (Gazelles, Inc.,
2002), ix.

42 Ron Chernow, *Titan: The Life of John D. Rockefeller Sr.* (New York: Random
House Inc, 1998); Harnish, *Mastering the Rockefeller Habits*, 2002.

43 Keith R. McFarland, "Acknowledgements," in *The Breakthrough Company*,
1st ed. (New York: Random House, 2008).

44 McFarland, *Breakthrough Company*, 14.

45 Lencioni, *The Five Dysfunctions of a Team*, vii.

46 "#45 Jon Doerr," *Forbes*, last updated September 20, 2020,
https://www.forbes.com/profile/john-doerr/

47 John Doerr, *Measure What Matters* (New York: Portfolio/Penguin, 2018),
inside flap.

48 Doerr, *Measure What Matters*, 8.

Chapter 6

49 Marcel Schwantes, "Research Has Revealed the 5 Top Behaviors That
Fortune 500 Companies Like Apple, Amazon, and Microsoft Live By," Inc.,
August 8, 2019, https://www.inc.com/marcel-schwantes/research-has-re-
vealed-5-top-behaviors-thatfortune-500-companies-like-apple-amazon-
microsoft-live-by.html.

50   Patrick Lencioni, *The Advantage* (San Francisco: Jossey-Bass, 2012).

51   Lencioni, *The Advantage*, 95–98.

52   Verne Harnish, *Mastering the Rockefeller Habits* (New York: Gazelles, Inc., 2002), 44

53   Patrick Lencioni, *The Five Dysfunctions of a Team* (San Francisco: Jossey-Bass, 2002)

54   Michael E. Gerber, *The E-Myth Revisited* (New York: HarperCollins Publishers, 1995), Ch. 10.

55   Michael E. Gerber, *E-Myth Mastery* (New York: HarperCollins Publishers, 2005), 265.

Chapter 7

56   "Private SaaS Company Valuations: 2019," SaaS Capital, June 11, 2019, https://www.saas-capital.com/blog-posts/private-saas-company-valuations-2019/

57   Craig R. Everett, *2019 Private Capital Markets Report* (Malibu, CA: Pepperdine University Graziadio Business School, March 18, 2019), http://digitalcommons.pepperdine.edu/gsbm_pcm_pcmr/12

58   John Warrillow, *The Automatic Customer* (New York: Portfolio/Penguin, 2015.

59   "Reducing the Tax Impact on the Sale of Your Business," BNY Mellon, https://www.bnymellonwealth.com/articles/strategy/reducing-the-tax-impact-on-the-sale-of-your-business.jsp

60   "EU Merger Directive: Cross-Border Re-organisations," RKG Consulting, https://www.rkgconsulting.com/get-into-europe/eu-merger-directive-cross-border-re-organisations/

61   Investopedia Staff, "Asset Protection Trust (APT)," Investopedia, updated June 20, 2020, https://www.investopedia.com/terms/a/asset-protection- trust.asp

Chapter 8

62   John Warrillow, *Built to Sell* (New York: Portfolio/Penguin, 2010).

63   Aswath Damodaran, "Valuing Acquisitions—Create Operating or Financial Synergy," Performance Trading, https://www.performancetrading.it/Documents/AdValuing/AdV_Create.htm

64   W. Chan Kim and Renée Mauborgne, "Blue Ocean Strategy," *Harvard Business Review*, October 2004.

65   "Industries with the Fastest Growing and Most Rapidly Declining Wage and Salary Employment," US Bureau of Labor Statistics, last modified September 1, 2020, https://www.bls.gov/emp/tables/industries-fast-grow-decline-employment.htm

66   "Chapter 7: Declining Markets: Characteristics & Strategies for Companies," in Business 327: Retail Strategy online course, Study.com, https://study.com/academy/lesson/declining-markets-characteristics-strategies-for-companies.html

67   "Disruption Need Not Be an Enigma," Accenture, February 26, 2018, https://www.accenture.com/_acnmedia/PDF-72/Accenture-Disruptability-Index-POV-Final.pdf.

68   Jim Collins, *Great by Choice* (New York: HarperCollins, 2011), chap. 6

69   Joe Panettieri, "What's Your SMaC Business Recipe for Success?" Channel Futures, November 13, 2012, https://www.channelfutures.com/sales-marketing/whats-your-smac-business-recipe-for-success

70   Collins, *Great by Choice*, chaps. 3, 6.

71   Clara Lu, "Apple Supply Chain—the Best Supply Chain in the World," Trade Gecko, April 15, 2020, https://www.tradegecko.com/blog/supply-chain-management/apple-the-best-supply-chain-in-the-world

72   Laurence Frost, Andreas Cremer, and Paul Lienert, "Volkswagen's Mega-platform Strategy the Holy Grail of Car Makers," *Globe and Mail*, February 11, 2013, https://www.theglobeandmail.com/globe-drive/news/volkswagens-mega-platform-strategy-the-holy-grail-of-car-makers/article8459298/

Chapter 9

73   Iris Dorbian, "Firefly Acquires EOS," PE Hub, June 6, 2018, https://www.pehub.com/firefly-acquires-eos/.

74   Chris Zook and James Allen, "Growth Outside the Core," *Harvard Business Review*, December 2003, https://hbr.org/2003/12/growth-outside-the-core

75   Fabienne Cretin, Stéphane Dieudonné, and Slimane Bouacha, "M&A Activity: Where Are We in the Cycle?" *Alternative Investment Analyst Review*, Summer 2015, 38–44, https://caia.org/aiar/access/article-937

76   Julian Gavaghan and Lydia Warren, "Instagram's 13 Employees Share $100m as CEO Set to Make $400m Reveals He Once Turned Down a Job at Facebook," *Daily Mail*, April 9, 2012, https://www.dailymail.co.uk/news/article-2127343/Facebook-buys-Instagram-13-employees-share-100m-CEO-Kevin-Systrom-set-make-400m.html

Chapter 10

77   Laura Cooper, "Bregal Sagemount Invests in Software Maker Corcentric,"
     Wall Street Journal, May 6, 2020, https://www.wsj.com/articles/bregal-sage-
     mount-invests-in-software-maker-corcentric-11588716216

78   "A Comprehensive Guide to ESOPs," Crowe, May 20, 2016, https://www.
     crowe.com/insights/asset/a/a-comprehensive-guide-to-esops

79   "Considering an IPO? First, Understand the Costs," PwC, https://www.
     pwc.com/us/en/services/deals/library/cost-of-an-ipo.html

INDEX

Made in the USA
Columbia, SC
03 May 2024

35215521R00171